Lost *on a* Familiar Road

*Allowing God's Love
to Free Your Mind
for the Journey*

New Hope Books by

Kimberly Sowell

Journey to Confidence: Becoming Women Who Witness

Journey to Significance: Becoming Women of Divine Destiny

*A Month of Miracles: 30 Stories of the
Unmistakable Presence of God* (coauthor)

Soul Shaping: Creating Compassionate Children

*Women of the Covenant: Spiritual Wisdom
from Women of the Bible* (coauthor)

Chosen and Cherished: Becoming the Bride of Christ
(coauthor)

A Passion for Purpose: 365 Daily Devotions for Missional Living
(coauthor)

*Major Truths from the Minor Prophets: Power,
Freedom, and Hope for Women* (coauthor)

Lost *on a* Familiar Road

Allowing God's Love to Free Your Mind for the Journey

kimberly sowell

NEW HOPE
PUBLISHERS
Gospel-Centered. Missions-Driven.

BIRMINGHAM, ALABAMA

New Hope® Publishers
P. O. Box 12065
Birmingham, AL 35202-2065
NewHopeDigital.com
New Hope Publishers is a division of WMU®.

Library of Congress Cataloging-in-Publication Data

Sowell, Kimberly.
  Lost on a familiar road : allowing God's love to free your mind for the
journey / Kimberly Sowell.
     p. cm.
  ISBN 978-1-59669-360-9 (pbk.)
  1. Thought and thinking--Religious aspects--Christianity. I. Title.
  BV4598.4.S69 2013
  248.4--dc23
                          2012041767

ISBN-10: 1-59669-360-6
ISBN-13: 978-1-59669-360-9

N134103 • 0113 • 3M1

Dedication

To my dear husband, *Kevin*,
and three beautiful children, *Julia, Jay,* and *John Mark*,
I am blessed to walk the road of life with you.

Contents

Acknowledgments

One of the blessings of life is to connect with people who are like-minded and who work together for a common goal. I am privileged to work with New Hope Publishers, a publishing company dedicated to doing everything excellently as unto the Lord. I wish to extend a special word of thanks to the staff of New Hope for their focus on Christ and His kingdom. New Hope, your desire to be more than simply another publishing company has been noted; you are shining forth the light of Jesus Christ, and I thank you for the honor of working with you.

—Kimberly

A Personal Note to You the Reader

Lost on a Familiar Road

I woke up one day and was keenly aware that I wasn't where I had been before. There was this niggling sensation that a subtle shift had taken place in my world, and it was leaving me restless.

I felt slightly different, and it wasn't a good kind of different. I was neither tearful nor depressed. I was neither happy nor unhappy. I wasn't numb, but I also wasn't geared up to tackle the day as I sorted through random thoughts about my life. So, what was this odd sensation blanketing my mind and causing me to feel unsettled?

In every drawer of the file cabinet of my mind, matters appeared to be in order. My family was healthy and my children were growing beautifully. My husband and I had a strong marriage. My ministry was rolling along in the right direction, and I sensed God's hand of favor in my work. I was in God's Word daily and hearing God's voice. The basic details were the same, and in the same thought, every detail seemed slightly askew. Nothing major had changed. No new job, no family transitions, no health concerns, no crises, and no life-changing disruptions. Everything was normal. How bizarre to look around and feel as if nothing in my life had changed, and yet something was amiss. It was almost like I could step back and watch this person named Kimberly living my life and feel so tempted to give her a check mark by her name on the list of people experiencing a fulfilling life, but . . . she wasn't quite convincing me; she seemed to be faking it a little bit.

I couldn't figure out how to fix my problem because I really didn't know how to define the problem. Was I just in a funk? I could live with my today, but I knew in my heart that my today was lacking—it could be so much more! I was sure of it because I had thrived on higher planes in times past. Nothing was terrible . . . just not satisfying. It was almost as if I felt I was no longer sure just where I belonged in my own life. I was lost on a familiar road.

Familiarity is not a bad thing. It's an ingredient that can help you thrive in your groove. You know who you are, you know whose you are, you know what you're here to do, and you know how to get it done. Then you do it. Every day, all day long, you can look unto Jesus, keeping your eyes on the prize, because you can function with precision in your familiar surroundings. It requires less thinking or studying because you can shift a portion of your brain into autopilot and just go with it, focusing only on that which demands the lion's share of your attention. But what happens when autopilot starts to get uncomfortable? What do you do when you sit down on the curb on your familiar road, study your surroundings, and then find yourself asking, "Now, God . . . remind me again what it is that I'm doing here. Is this the right path? Am I fulfilling whatever it is that You have for me to do, and if so, could You remind me how to do this in a way that glorifies You? I know where I am, but I'm feeling a little lost, Lord." And that's what happened to me.

One day, all of this laborious chatter in my brain about feeling lost on my familiar road was transpiring in one of the most beautiful, tranquil locations on the earth: I was sitting on the beach as the sun began to set, with warm, gentle pools of water washing over my toes. *Wow, am I in trouble if I can't feel settled in my mind at the beach!* I strummed the sand mindlessly with my fingers, reaching out for nothing in particular, when I happened upon an ordinary shell. I picked up the little clam shell and examined its detail, finding it unimpressive. In my bleak outlook, I first noticed its uneven shape and discoloration, not to mention the heavy wear and tear this shell had endured that wore down it's striations into smooth boringness. But with a slight turn of my wrist, I noticed that a small portion of the shell had been sheltered from the elements, and its striations and grooves were fully intact and inspiring. Partly worn down, partly strong and unscathed. *Just like me,* I thought. The Lord saw the worn down side of me, and He knew in detail the process that had occurred that had worn down my uniqueness over time. And yet I hoped there was still a part of me that was fresh and untouched, uniquely me and vibrant. I turned the shell over in my hands and studied its form from every angle. *Are you sure which side of the shell you admire? Are you right to value the untouched side over the smooth? Choose a side, Kimberly.* I decided to take the shell home. The little gray broken hull was a beautiful image of my own brokenness and my need to rediscover my place on this familiar road that was my life.

When we find ourselves in need of direction, we need only to look into God's Word as our user-friendly guide to life. As I sought God's face for help, He navigated me to this basic yet foundational directive from Jesus: *"And you shall love the Lord your God with all your heart, with all your soul, with all your mind, and with all your strength.' This is the first commandment"* (Mark 12:30). I began to examine my habits, and what I discovered through this journey was that this sensation of restlessness or

11

unsettledness wasn't about what I was or wasn't *doing*, but it was about what I was *thinking*; I was loving God with my hands, my feet, my resources, perhaps even with my heart, soul, and strength, but I had not learned to love God completely with my mind. My thoughts were defeating me, because they weren't under the lordship of Christ. I had to learn not only to submit my mind to God, but also to use my mind to glorify God in every secret place of my brain where thoughts are entertained, ideas are considered, and decisions are made.

If you're feeling restless, or perhaps even just a little out of sorts, don't despair. You're not alone. The decision to make right now is that you'll not wander off the path that God has for you. Don't run with your restlessness; that would be akin to spiritually running with scissors! Stay put and let God direct you on this path. And as you learn to love God with your mind, you'll love God like you've never loved Him before. Your mind will be doing what it was created to do, fully functioning and fueled with God's love. Your mind will grow freer, stronger, sharper, and energized. Let God change your mind. The restlessness will fade away, and you will thrive again as you stroll along your familiar road.

12

chapter one
What's on Your Mind?

You will keep him in perfect peace,
Whose mind is stayed on You,
Because he trusts in You.
—Isaiah 26:3—

"*What's on your mind?" It is one of the most legitimate questions ever posed, because it's impossible to know what a person is thinking unless she chooses to reveal her thoughts. Often we aren't even aware of our own thoughts, but these brain vibes are affecting our moment-by-moment decisions. We string those decisions together, and we call it life.*

Every noble act, every amazing discovery, and every evil scheme shaping human history was first birthed in the mind of someone willing to indulge the thought. You are capable of greatness for the glory of God. Knowing the potential outcomes of every man's thinking, answer carefully: "What's on your mind?"

DAY 1: BRAIN CLUTTER

Thought: A brain daily challenged with multitasking overload
is too cluttered to focus on loving God.

Challenge: Allow God to bring focus and clarity to your thinking.

You're dashing toward the living room with a spatula in one hand and a stack of newspapers in the other, and your mind is racing with a mental to-do list: *I've got to finish these chores, then I'll have 20 minutes to scarf down supper, maybe I can get the bills paid before the meeting—oh! I'm out of stamps. OK, get to the post office when they open tomorrow and maybe my boss won't notice I'm a few minutes late. I've got to call that lady back about the committee position; oh, I hope I don't forget those stamps! I know I'm going to forget the stamps! Put the committee chair's phone number in my purse so I can call her on the way to my meeting. Does my cell phone need charging? My back is killing me, but there's no time to dig through the medicine cabinet*—and then you stop, dead in your tracks.

Your feet have arrived in the living room, but your brain has no idea what you've come for, though you're sure it's an item vital to your evening. You stand gazing across the room, scanning for something to jog your memory, all the while fretting about every second wasted because you just couldn't retain a simple thought like what you needed from the living room.

Sound familiar? And if so, where do you lay the blame for scatterbrained moments? That little edge of forgetfulness may be a sure sign that you've got too much on your mind. Perhaps you've got a problem—a brain clutter problem.

Over the next few days, be a casual observer of your fellow man. Take note of the pace people keep. Listen for phrases like, "I'm too busy," and "I've got to hurry." You might catch yourself saying words that carry this same common theme, and when you do, don't be surprised if your body begins feeling tense and your emotions run high. And what about your mind? In rat-race mode, are you loving God with your mind?

Consider a mind overflowing with people to call, messages to send, and chores to do, complimented nicely with one heaping spoonful of fear that you'll forget something important, alongside a healthy portion of guilt for all the people you're sure to disappoint when you do. Is this a mind that dwells on the loving-kindness of God (Psalm 48:9)? Could a person with such a mind say with integrity, *"My meditation [is] sweet to Him; I will be glad in the Lord"* (see Psalm 104:34.)?

What about clutter of another sort? In the day the Israelites gathered at Gilgal to make Saul their very first earthly king, there was much fanfare and rejoicing as the people made sacrifices of peace offerings before the Lord. Oh, the things they might have been thinking! Perhaps they were drunk with excitement, swimming in daydreams of conquests, jewels and riches, prestige, fame . . . but no thoughts of holy God, the King they were in affect rejecting when they demanded a flesh-and-blood king so they could be like the other peoples of the earth. Samuel, who had been their priest and judge, was present, and he knew with great sorrow how the Israelites tended to think. He knew their minds were cluttered with worldly thoughts, leaving little room for thoughts of the Almighty. Samuel stood before the people to redirect their thinking toward God. Samuel instructed the Israelites, *"Consider what great things He has done for you"* (1 Samuel 12:24). Samuel challenged them to stand still, stop thinking in the moment, and to know the truth by focusing on the amazing love and grace God had poured upon them and their people.

When you focus your thinking on God's goodness, suddenly everything changes. You can see the clutter for what it is. You can detect worldliness. Busyness that you've been clutching

15

tightly to your chest suddenly seems of little worth and you gladly lay it aside. Such vital consideration of the faithfulness of God is enough to keep your mind occupied all day long, and you gladly trade in the exhausting mental to-do lists for joyful thoughts of Christ.

If you can't afford the brain space to be actively thinking of God's goodness today, your mind—and your life—are too cluttered. Perhaps you agree with this assessment but see no reasonable way to simplify your life. Begin here: God doesn't need you to be so busy that your brain stays frazzled. God doesn't measure your worth by the number of proverbial plates you keep spinning in motion. What God has called you to do, He will equip and strengthen you to do at a healthy pace. Is the Christian life meant to be mentally challenging? Yes. Is the Christian life meant to be mentally exhausting? Ask the Lord to give you the correct answer to that question.

Time to Think:

1. What percent of my mind is filled with clutter?

   _____ percent

   What percent is filled with sweet thoughts of Christ?

   _____ percent

2. How often do I feel stressed out about my daily schedule?

   ❑ 1–2 times a day   ❑ 3–5 times a day

   ❑ throughout most of the day

   During these times, am I loving God with my mind? Am I projecting my love for God to others?

3. When my life is filled with busyness, what is usually the cause?

   _____ I can't tell people no because I don't want to hurt their feelings. (pride)

   _____ I don't think anyone else can do the task as well as I can. (pride)

   _____ I like to keep a hectic pace. (lunacy?)

   _____ I don't allow myself time to pray about and think about decisions. (impatience)

4. What can I do *today* to declutter my mind?

5. What are two truths about God that I want to meditate on today?

   1) _____

   2) _____

   Don't be surprised when all of these wonderful God thoughts fill your heart as well as your mind, and you find yourself having to tell someone about God's goodness today.

17

What Was Jethro Thinking?

Exodus 18

It was going to be one of those days that most men only dreamed about. Jethro proudly escorted his daughter Zipporah and his two grandsons back home to their father, Moses, who had returned victoriously from what had to be the most spectacular display of God's sovereign power that Jethro could imagine. Moses was still the humble man Jethro remembered, as Moses greeted his father-in-law by bowing down and offering him a kiss. The aged Jethro bent his ear to every detail of the mind-blowing, history-altering victory of the Israelites, as Moses told the tales with a gleam in his eye. God's people had broken free from Egypt's bondage under the leadership of Moses; oh, the pride of a father-in-law for his son-in-law who set a nation free and also lovingly cares for his family and for his beloved daughter, Zipporah! Jethro cried out, *"Blessed be the Lord, who has delivered you out of the hand of the Egyptians and out of the hand of Pharaoh, and who has delivered the people from under the hand of the Egyptians"* (v. 10). Yes, it was going to be a good visit with the in-laws.

But the very next day, Jethro's heart grew concerned for Moses as he witnessed the people standing in the sun from morning to evening, waiting to get counsel from Moses. Every Israelite had access to Moses for any and all matters, and Jethro realized that this excessive burden was going to clutter his son-in-law's life. *"The thing that you do is not good,"* said Jethro (v. 17). Moses was God's chosen leader for Israel, but he didn't have to—and couldn't—do it all by himself. Jethro spoke up to help

18

his son-in-law, teaching him to declutter his life and averting a potential crash-and-burn for Moses.

Highly effective Christians realize that maintaining mental health is vital to success. They declutter their minds by prioritizing, delegating, and living within the boundaries of what one human can do with God's strength. They love God with a mind that has made room for thoughts, dreams, and wisdom from above as they meditate on God's goodness. Find a "Jethro" and ask for his or her perspective on what is cluttering your life.

DAY 2: TAKE OUT THE TRASH

Thought: God cares about the contents of our thought life. He has prescribed uplifting thoughts to fill our minds.

19

Challenge: Replace negativity with uplifting thinking in obedience to Christ.

I hadn't bothered to go in my basement for a few weeks, but when I finally decided to relax in our family's little cave, the smell hit me as soon as I reached the bottom stair—we needed to take out the trash! Trash invites all sorts of problems. It stinks, it takes up space, and if left unattended, it can breed some disgusting houseguests. Negative thoughts are aptly described as mind trash.

Are you in a situation that has led to troubled thinking? The Apostle Paul was no stranger to the anxieties of life, having experienced threats against his life, pain and sorrows, and imprisonment. God nurtured Paul through these experiences, and as a result, Paul was qualified to offer this set of instructions in Philippians 4:6–7 about overcoming anxiety with prayer: "*Be anxious for nothing, but in everything by prayer and supplication, with thanksgiving, let your requests be made known to God; and the peace of God, which surpasses all understanding, will guard your hearts and minds through Christ Jesus.*" There's a process to follow: Take the problem to God, season your words with thanksgiving, and then watch God's peace establish a protective force field to shield your mind from further anxiety.

Try to capture this image that Paul has painted. Your mind is a globular mass with multiple entry points, vulnerable on all sides. But every day, a shield of peace forms to protect your mind because you pray to God and hand your problems over to the Almighty. Satan relentlessly tries to penetrate your mind with negative thoughts, but God's peace holds firm. A doubt about your parenting rises up against you, but it bounces off like rubber against God's shield of peace. An anxious thought about this month's bills tries to bombard your mind, but God's peace quickly moves in on this thought and they melt away. No matter which fiery dart Satan throws at you, He cannot bring you to despair because God's peace wins. Even on a day when you feel quivery and weak-minded, you can rest secure behind God's shield of peace when you've prayed with thanksgiving, making your requests known to God. Once you've given a burden to the Lord, what will you think about? What should be happening in that gray matter as it operates behind the shield of peace? Paul has the answer: "*Finally, brethren, whatever things are true, whatever things are noble, whatever things are just, whatever things are pure, whatever things are lovely, whatever things are of good report, if there is any virtue and if there is anything praiseworthy—meditate on these things*" (Philippians 4:8).

Is this "the power of positive thinking"? Absolutely not. Paul's instructions aren't attached to a promise that you can think yourself well or prosperous. It's more a matter of faith. Once you've poured out your troubles to the Lord, move on in your mind and meditate on the things that will keep your heart singing on a dark day:

- Instead of discouraging stories that you aren't sure are true, think on what is certain to be true.
- Instead of what is shameful, think on what is noble.
- Instead of injustice, justice.
- Instead of that which is tainted, focus on that which is pure.
- Instead of the ugly, think on the lovely.
- Instead of that which deserves a poor evaluation, think on that which is worthy of good report.
- Instead of the worthless and deplorable, think on the virtuous and praiseworthy.

21

What a contrast! And why on earth would you even be tempted to think on ugly matters? Could it be that you're bombarded with negative comments, gossip, bad news, and displays of poor behavior so often that the trash begins to heap up in your brain? While you cannot be immune to negative information, you can be proactive to walk away from destructive conversations. And what about a simple step like filling your ears with worship music that will keep your mind focused on the goodness of the Lord? Throughout the day, take out the trash.

Is this positive kind of thinking a step you're willing to take? Be alert about your thinking today; you may be surprised how often you feel the need to take out the trash. When you find yourself mulling over negative thoughts, switch your focus to the blessings of Christ. Worship Him and offer Him your love as you fill your mind with thoughts worthy of your King.

Time to Think:

1. Is it possible to love God with my mind if my thoughts are typically negative?

2. Am I a negative person? Do I lift people up or pull them down with my words?

3. What do I think about when I'm alone?

4. What am I typically thinking about as I lie in bed each night, waiting to fall asleep?

5. Am I attracted to bad news and gossip, or do I prefer good news about others' lives?

6. What are two truths I can dwell on today that fit the parameters of thinking prescribed in Philippians 4:8?

What Was Noah Thinking?

Genesis 6–7

"Noah walked with God" (6:9). When the Bible describes a man as just and blameless, and he had a relationship with the Lord, you have an inkling about his thought life. Noah wasn't perfect, but in an era when *"the* LORD *saw that the wickedness of man was great in the earth, and that every intent of the thoughts of his heart was only evil continually"* (6:5) . . . *"Noah found grace in the eyes of the* LORD*"* (6:8). Noah was a righteous man.

So as Noah receded into the bowels of safety of this massive vessel he had been building for the last 100 years, what was he thinking? As he listened to the howling wind and the beating of the rain against gopher wood, how was his mental health? We don't know if Noah could see or hear the throngs of men, women, boys, and girls as they spewed evil until their final, dying, drowning breaths, but either way, Noah knew about the carnage taking place on the other side of the lumber. His mind was aware. Noah lived through one of the most horrific tragedies in human history.

After the water rose and the cries for help were nothing but memories, Noah was alone with his thoughts. Sure, he had animals to tend and a family to lead, but Noah had nothing but time as he waited months for the rain to end and the waters to recede. Perhaps Noah had learned mental toughness from 100 years of enduring scorn and ridicule as he built the ark; perhaps there were days while he pounded the nails that he thought about the day of retribution that was coming for those who mocked him, when the truth would be revealed, and Noah begged God to guard his mind from evil thoughts of revenge.

23

But in the ark, there was no more speculation, because now the scoffers had been silenced and nothing would ever be the same.

Noah had been given an awesome task: to live on. He and his family were commissioned to replenish the earth and be the roots of God's new beginning for mankind. Noah couldn't afford to entertain thoughts of despair about the past or negativity about the present because his future was too important, and each day was an opportunity to love God with his mind.

You, too, have an awesome task: to make the most of your today. You can't begin to fathom how much your mind has to do with the success of this day. Fuel your mind with wholesome, God-ordained thoughts, and reject negativity.

24

DAY 3: SPIRITUAL PERSPECTIVE

Thought: As followers of Christ, our calling is to see things as Christ sees them—to adopt Christ's perspective on the world.

Challenge: Express your love for God by taking a Christian perspective on each thought, attitude, and decision.

Perspective is golden. Seventeen cents is of little value to a banker, but it makes a three-year-old feel like a bazillionaire. A biscuit is a meager meal, unless you're an ant. An hour flies by for children enjoying recess, but it seems like an eternity for a woman in labor.

Perspective—how you view the world—shapes your decision-making process. Your perspective has likely changed through the years because experiences, relationships, age, and life situations help shape your thinking. These outside influences are the very reason that you must choose wisely about the movies you watch, the company you keep, and the places you go, because each story you see played out before your eyes, each conversation, each life experience, is battling to sway your opinion. You can harness this power of influence to work to your advantage by submersing yourself in situations that will shape your perspective for the good, but the greatest influence on your perspective must be Jesus Christ.

Jesus saw the world differently than the people around Him. Even though His disciples were near Him, they often struggled to understand Christ's teachings because their perspectives had been tainted by years of sitting under the tutelage of the world. One day the disciples came to Christ and asked, *"Who then is greatest in the kingdom of heaven'"* (Matthew 18:1)? The Romans would have answered that question from a pagan's perspective; would they have said that the greatest is the one who is champion on the battlefield or the stealthiest strategist in the military tent? The Pharisees would have responded based on their legalistic perspective; would they have praised the one who was the chief law-keeper among law-keepers? But Jesus answered with the perspective of the King of the kingdom of heaven. He placed a child in their midst and answered, *"Unless you are converted and become as little children, you will by no means enter the kingdom of heaven. Therefore whoever humbles himself as this little child is the greatest in the kingdom of heaven"* (18:3–4). Jesus extolled humility; the greatest in God's kingdom are those who are willing to be like children, to strip away layer upon layer of the world's carnal influences, to put aside all of the world's wisdom and stop relying on how smart we think we are, and to be molded and shaped anew by Christ.

As Christians, *"we have the mind of Christ"* (1 Corinthians 2:16). This gift is given to every believer from God Himself. The mind of Christ is beyond ability to describe in its greatness, but as it applies to perspective, it might be described as an invaluable filtering system that helps you evaluate information with the attitude of Christ, or as a special lens that allows your eyes to see the world through the eyes of Christ.

If you're a believer, does this mean that you already have Christ's perspective? Not necessarily.

Truly operating with the mind of Christ takes prayer, intentionality, and spiritual discipline, because Christ's perspective doesn't come naturally to us. Christ's way of thinking is in direct opposition with the world and even with our own flesh, so taking Christ's perspective means that we must choose to allow God to overrule our weaker ways of thinking. Think about it: for those who do not have the mind of Christ, the Christian worldview seems foolish. Christ calls us to love unconditionally, give sacrificially, and live uprightly regardless of the consequences; from the perspective of our flesh, that sounds like a miserable life, but from Christ's perspective working in us to win over our minds, it's a glorious way to live! Therefore, Paul wrote, *"Let this mind be in you which was also in Christ Jesus"* (Philippians 2:5). Having the mind of Christ is a gift; yielding to the mind of Christ is a choice.

You are filtering data throughout each day, reeling in new information, formulating opinions, and choosing how you'll respond. Yield to the mind of Christ today. Take on His perspective. Look into the eyes of your family, friends, and even strangers, and see them through Christ's eyes. Respond to challenges just as Christ would have you respond. Spiritual perspective will result in godly thinking, godly thinking will result in godly actions, and godly actions will result in glory for God's kingdom. Are you ready to see things Christ's way today? It will make for some interesting thinking.

Time to Think:

1. Does my perspective on holy conduct and speech line up with the mind of Christ?

2. As I think of the people in my sphere of influence who are spiritually lost, what are the thoughts I have been thinking about these individuals lately? Does my thinking match the way Jesus views the lost of this world?

27

3. What is God's perspective on interacting with my enemies? Am I dealing with difficult people with that same perspective?

4. Is there any area of my life in which I know my perspective is not in line with Christ's, but I'm unwilling to yield to the mind of Christ? If so, why?

5. *"For My thoughts are not your thoughts, nor are your ways My ways," says the Lord"* (Isaiah 55:8). Apart from the Savior, no one is capable of having a godly perspective. Do I make a conscientious attempt to detect when my thoughts and ways have strayed from being under the authority of Christ?

What Was Peter Thinking?

Matthew 16:21–28

Peter had met the Christ, the Son of the living God; he was convinced of it (v. 16). Peter had been an eyewitness as Jesus healed the sick, cast out demons, and raised the dead. Peter knew that Jesus had command over the earth and its natural elements, and even Peter himself had taken a stroll on the crashing waves with the Master. Peter had sat under Christ's teachings and marveled as Jesus confounded His accusers while touching the hearts of the common man. Peter was there when Jesus miraculously fed the multitudes, and he surrendered to Christ's authority when Jesus commissioned Peter and the other 11 disciples with power over unclean spirits and disease. Yes, Jesus' ministry was well underway, and the Messiah's plan was unfolding nicely.

But then Jesus began to say things that seemed contrary to that plan. Jesus began telling Peter and the others that *"He must go to Jerusalem and suffer many things from the elders and chief priests and scribes, and be killed, and be raised the third day"* (v. 21). Peter thought He was on the same wavelength with Christ, but now Jesus seemed to be veering off course. Everything was going so well! Why change course now? Why ruin this good thing? Peter took Jesus aside; did he think Jesus had lost focus? Did he think that for the first time, Jesus was about to steer them wrong? Peter said to the Lord, *"Far be it from You, Lord; this shall not happen to You"* (v. 22)!

Note Jesus didn't thank Peter for his concern and friendship. Jesus didn't grin and tell Peter, "You'll see." Jesus viewed Peter's lack of perspective as a direct assault against the kingdom of

God. *"Get behind Me, Satan! You are an offense to Me, for you are not mindful of the things of God, but the things of men'"* (v. 23). After all this time, Peter still wasn't seeing the ministry from Christ's perspective; he was seeing it from a carnal perspective. Peter loved Jesus, but Peter's way of thinking was not only wrong, it was dangerous and of the devil.

You love the Lord. You walk with Him. So did Peter, but Peter still didn't see the big picture because Peter wanted to define success as the world defines success. What do you need to see through the eyes of Jesus today?

DAY 4: A BALANCED DIET FOR THE BRAIN

Thought: God created us to thrive on a well-balanced life-style, which includes a variety of opportunities to use our minds in a productive manner.

Challenge: Make time for creativity, dreaming, learning, and working.

There's a saying about all work and no play, but Jack's not the only one who struggles to stay well-balanced. How curious that every woman has her own bent; some of us lean toward too much work, others are heavy on the girlfriend time, while other women have treasure troves of dreams that will never become reality because their hands never seem to get around to step one of making dreams come true.

I also tend to lean out of balance. I've been accused of being a "ministry-aholic." I've created a new monster, and it's me! For years I felt that working and doing ministry from sunup to sundown was God's best for me, and the void of friendships and leisure activity was a sign of my commitment to God. But I woke up one day and realized I had gotten rusty at good girl talk; I couldn't be anyone's best friend even if I tried. With further exploration, I detected a chronic fatigue in my body I had been ignoring for some time. And not only was my body tired, but my mind was tired. My creative juices were all but depleted. I sat at my computer and begged God for one original thought, but I couldn't hack out one pithy sentence on my keyboard. Worst of all, think time was not a luxury I had indulged in for quite awhile, and my dreams were tapped out. I had lost sight of where God was taking me, because I had kept my nose to the grindstone for too long, where the view was short and the dreams were suppressed for another day that I had never gotten around to taking.

30

What drives us to play too much or work too hard? Why is balance so difficult? The answer is sin. Perhaps the chronic daydreamer struggles in her faith, preferring to keep her head in the clouds rather than take a risk. Maybe the socialite struggles with low self-esteem, securing her identity from what others think of her rather than finding her identity in Christ. For me, I worked too often because of pride; I somehow felt like God "needed" my services so much that there wasn't time to care for my health or nurture my brain to keep both healthy and strong. I meant well, but I had weakened my ability to love God with my mind.

David was the king of Israel. Who had more to do than David? David's responsibilities were great, and every person in the kingdom was counting on him. But remember that this man of great power and responsibility penned some of the most beloved verses of comfort: *"The Lord is my shepherd; I shall not want. He makes me to lie down in green pastures; He leads me beside the still waters. He restores my soul"* (Psalm 23:1–3). Not only was David allowing God to shepherd him as a leader, but

God was drawing David aside for rest, refreshing, and renewal. The most important man in the kingdom took time to lie in the grass, look over the waters, and breathe deeply as God restored what the world had emptied from him. No wonder David was able to run a kingdom, succeed on the battlefield, and also write beautiful psalms that drip with God's glory.

Jesus is always our best example. What Jesus valued, we must also value. While He walked among men on earth, Jesus modeled a balanced life. What did that look like for the Son of God? Jesus' childhood was characterized in this way: *"And Jesus increased in wisdom and stature, and in favor with God and men"* (Luke 2:52). Jesus maintained balance in His growth. We have very little detail in Scripture about His growing-up experiences, but an increase in wisdom tells us that He stayed in God's Word. An increase in stature tells us that He didn't neglect exercise and nutrition. Increase in favor with God tells us His relationship with His Father was first priority. Increase in favor with men tells us that Jesus forged relationships with people that were healthy and productive. Once Jesus had grown to be a man and began His earthly ministry, He went to a wedding, observed feasts, shared a fish fry with friends on the shore, pulled away to pray, ministered passionately, taught the multitudes, and invested in others on a personal level. Jesus was always focused and on task, and somehow "on task" even included sharing a final observance of the Passover supper with His disciples and friends the evening before going to the Cross. Jesus maintained balance. Jesus knew He had only roughly three years to complete His ministry and that each person on the face of the earth was in desperate need of His healing touch, yet the overwhelming need didn't throw Jesus off balance. He still pulled aside to pray, He didn't rush through conversations, He blessed little children. . . . He was the perfect picture of the balanced life.

31

If we're going to learn to love God with our minds, we're going to need this same balance. It's like building the perfect sandcastle with sand and water—too much of either ingredient makes for flimsy walls, but the ideal blend of sand and water makes a solid, brilliant structure. We also need to hit that ideal balance to be solid in body, mind, and spirit. The experiences we gain from friendships and leisure will enhance our creativity and expand our mental abilities. Rest will boost our energy, strengthen our minds, and build our faith that God has indeed given us enough hours in a day to complete our assignments. Time to think, pray, and dream with God will open our minds to God's direction and bolster discernment.

Sounding good? Give the balanced brain diet a try. Your brain just might hug you for it, and your renewed mind will be able to love God at a greater capacity than ever before.

Time to Think:

1. Where do I tend to gravitate—focusing on work, leisure, exercise, or some other activity? What area of my life receives the greatest neglect?

2. How often do I carve out time to sit still and think?

3. How often do I engage in mindless activities, like watching TV? During those times, what is my mind receiving from those mindless experiences?

33

4. How am I exercising creativity?

5. How could a lifestyle adjustment enhance what my mind is able to do, allowing my mind to love God more fervently?

What Was Martha Thinking?

Luke 10:38–42

She was a committed follower of Christ. She probably knew what a big deal it was that Jesus was visiting her home. I don't think Jesus chose to stop at this particular house in Bethany because of its convenient location, or because the cushions were the best in town, or because the cooking was almost as good as His mother's. I doubt Martha thought that, either, but it was these kinds of matters of hospitality that Martha wanted to have perfect for Jesus. These things arrested her attention and kept her from sitting beside Mary at the feet of Jesus to listen to His word.

Martha was *"distracted"* (v. 40), which can be translated, *drawn away from.* To be drawn away from means Martha was supposed to be in one location, but she ended up being somewhere else. She was supposed to be at Jesus' feet, listening to Him and spending time with this Guest in her home who was also her Lord, but she was drawn away by something else. What was it? She was *"distracted with much serving"* (v. 40). It was figs, or flat bread, pitchers of water or the like, that drew her away from this much needed time of fellowship with the Lord.

What is distracting you? And what are you being drawn away from? What is that place that you never seem to get around to because you're busy with other demands? For Martha, it was *"that good part"* (v. 42). Whether it's your pillow, a winding country road, flower beds, or the wicker chair in the sunroom where you used to do daily devotions, reclaim that place by believing that God loves you enough to give you balance.

DAY 5: KEEP TALKING

Thought: Communicating with God throughout the day leads to accurate thinking and sound decisions.

Challenge: Discipline your mind to communicate with God regularly.

We don't want to admit it, but we're all guilty of this quirky mind activity more than we even realize. The person we talk to most often throughout each day is ourselves. I've had meaningful conversations with myself on long car rides, which seems reasonable or at least forgivable, but I occasionally talk to myself even while having a conversation with other people. It's inexcusable, really, but my saving grace is that no one knows when I'm silently cutting him or her off midsentence because what I have to say to myself at that moment seems far more pressing and deserving of my attention. I can only hope that a glazed look isn't crossing my face in those momentary lapses, giving away the truth about my secret interruption.

When we have the option, we tend to talk with people whose ideas we value and perspectives we appreciate. When I have a child-rearing issue, my mother's phone is going to ring. When sports, politics, or financial issues arise, my husband is my go-to person. For the toughest situations requiring careful navigation, my dad is a steady source of advice. So why do I consult myself for the majority of my decisions each day? Why do I keep talking to myself when I could be talking to God?

I have not earned a very good track record on giving advice to myself. I've talked myself into ruining a perfectly beautiful day by wallowing in self-pity. I once convinced myself that pouting and door-slamming would somehow make my husband a better person. (I was proven wrong.) Need I revisit the time my mind was sure that singing karaoke was a good idea? Thus, my own self is probably not the person I should consult on a regular basis. After all, God calls the heart *"deceitful above all things"* (Jeremiah 17:9 NIV), and beyond my personal understanding. In other words, I'm fully capable of fooling myself! However, my heavenly Father is the ultimate Communication Partner. God further states in Jeremiah 17:10 (NIV), *"I the Lord search the heart and examine the mind."* When I talk with God throughout the day instead of talking to myself, He sifts through my self-deception and is Master of my mind. He straightens out any crooked thinking and illuminates my mind with His love and light.

Prayer is a critical component of loving God with the mind, and we are called to *"continue earnestly in prayer"* (Colossians 4:2). When we pray, our communication with God trumps all thinking, because God is shaping our thoughts with His message to us. We desperately need to hear from God, and we must listen carefully, because we cannot afford to miss *a single word*. Why? Because God's words are powerful. God spoke, and creation happened. Jesus spoke and called the dead back to life. Every word that God speaks is holy, true, and life-giving. His words are eternal, and He wants to talk to us. In fact, He is willing to speak directly into our lives, if we'll only free up our minds from the mindless self-chatter in order to focus our full attention upon the voice of Holy God.

One of my greatest epiphanies about my prayer life has to do with my tendency toward three-way communication. I already knew I was talking to God (one). I knew God was talking to me (two). But what was startling to realize was that I also am sometimes talking to myself (three). I began to ask around and discovered that other people have similar prayer woes. Not sure if you're guilty? During those times, the conversation goes something like this: "God, thank You for helping me finish that project on time. Please, God, speak to the hearts of the women who will receive those blankets and a gospel witness at the prison." (Next, God washes over me with His assurance.) "And, God, please bless the prison guard, Helga. Thank You that she professes Christ as her Savior; and, God, please help her be kind and compassionate to the inmates each day." (God responds with encouragement.) Then I begin to talk to myself: *Helga was so rude to me last week, and she snapped at one of the other guards. Should I pray about that? But maybe I'm judging her. Did I just misunderstand what she said? Maybe she just has a tough exterior because she works with inmates. I wonder if deep down, Helga is afraid of the inmates. Maybe I should take Helga that book on courage. That reminds me! I was supposed to return that book to the library last week. I wonder if my children have any overdue books . . .* and off I go into my own little conversation with me, myself, and I. Sound familiar? These mental side trips are further evidence that we need God to clear our minds and help us focus on Him when we pray. Scripture cautions: *"Do not be hasty in word or impulsive in thought to bring up a matter in the presence of God. For God is in heaven and you are on the earth; therefore let your words be few"* (Ecclesiastes 5:2 NASB). Looking at the whole of Scripture, this passage isn't teaching us to talk very little to God, but it does counsel us to make our words count.

New Age religion advocates emptying the mind, but the mind was not designed to lie dormant; the truth is that someone's always talking in your thoughts. Are you doing most of the talking? Talk up a storm, but talk with the One who knows all things and loves you with an everlasting love. Tell Him what's on your mind, and listen with a deep sense of awe as He deposits great truths into your mind.

Time to Think:

1. Is my prayer life consistent?

2. When I have good news, whom do I tell first? When a problem arises, whom do I tell first?

3. Does *"pray without ceasing"* (1 Thessalonians 5:17) sound impossible? Does it sound appealing to me?

4. Do I occasionally allow my personal opinions to trump God's Word? (Hint: It usually begins with the statement, "I know this is wrong, but . . .")

5. Do I ever tiptoe around subjects I would rather not pray about to God, because I don't want God to say what I don't want to hear?

6. How will I adjust my prayer habits to better love God with my mind?

What Were the Disciples Thinking?

Acts 1:12–14

Sometimes it just happens. I turn my face to the Lord for a fresh word, an insight, a niggle of inspiration, and I find myself staring at white walls. What happened? What did I do, and how can I undo it? I sit and wait, praying for God to paint a beautiful landscape to fill up the spiritual blank space, but what's in view is blinding whiteness. White walls. It's during these times that I struggle with the words to pray.

During a recent "white wall" experience, I thought, *Could this be how the disciples felt after Jesus departed?* After Jesus' resurrection, He spent time with the disciples and then ascended to the Father after 40 days. What now? Jesus told them to wait for the Promise of the Father (v. 4), so they waited, and prayed, along with Jesus' half brothers. Perhaps they prayed, "What now, Lord?"; or maybe they struggled to find the words to express to the Father how they were feeling. But then it happened: On the Day of Pentecost, the Holy Spirit came down, and these men who were privileged to walk with Jesus were now so filled with the movement of God in their lives, they could scarcely keep pace!

What can you do when you stare at white walls, waiting on God to speak? You can put yourself in a position of preparation. You can pray and wait with expectation, relishing this sweet reminder that you're fully dependent upon God at all times. You can thank the Lord, because you know He's working in unseen ways on your behalf, and grin with delight because you believe He's renewing your strength as you wait on Him (Isaiah 40:31). You can learn to appreciate white.

chapter two

The Battle Against Worry

Do not fret—it only causes harm.

—Psalm 37:8—

Worry can take our minds captive, and Jesus said it's a fruitless task: "Which of you by worrying can add one cubit to his stature" (Matthew 6:27)? Yet our minds are so frequently exercised on this very task of worrying, fretting, and fuming over our troubles, leaving us discouraged, depressed, or distracted at best.

Harm comes when we obsess about our problems—harm to our health, harm to our relationships, harm to our walk with Christ, and certainly harm to our ability to love God with our minds. The battle against worry—it's going to be a dog fight, but God can set our minds free to focus on Him.

DAY 6: BELIEVING BEYOND YOUR CIRCUMSTANCES

Thought: Personal circumstances may give the impression that our problems are going to overtake us, but God is not bound by our circumstances.

Challenge: Replace your thoughts about the overwhelming nature of your circumstances with thoughts about God's power and faithfulness.

"White milk? Daddy, you got me white milk? You know I like chocolate milk. Aw!" My six-year-old son, Jay, caved to his disappointment and began to pout. There was moaning and high-pitched despair, eye-rolling and a deep slump in Jay's shoulders because his daddy had gone through the drive-thru and returned with everybody's favorite burgers and fries, ruined for Jay because it would be washed down with white and not brown milk.

My husband retorted, "Jay, you need to hush. Just listen to me."

"No, Daddy, you got me white milk. I don't like it!"

"Jay, wait before you embarrass yourself."

On and on Jay moaned, pitching a doozy of a fit, until his daddy opened the bottle cap and we all peered inside to see brown milk inside the white milk container. "They were out of chocolate milk, Jay, so I asked them to put syrup in your milk to turn it into chocolate milk."

Jay's response: a sheepish "Oh."

On the surface, it appeared that all was lost, but inside the bottle was evidence that Jay's daddy had worked behind the scenes for his benefit to turn a bad situation into something very good. Jay knew all along how much his daddy loved him, but in that moment of weakness Jay focused on the circumstances he could see instead of remembering the kind heart of his daddy.

In our minds, we tell ourselves that God loves us and that He is in control. We pray and ask God to help us with our problems. But so often in our minds, the battle rages on after we say "amen" because we keep thinking about the circumstances and we sink into discouragement. The circumstances are the piles of bills we see with our eyes. They're the arguments we play over and over again in our minds when hurtful words were spoken. They're the pieces of the puzzle of our lives that we keep trying to put together, hoping they'll interlock to create to some sort of map to help us navigate our way out of a life maze, and the map we keep creating has a dead-end destination. When we doubt God during times of bleak circumstances, worry takes hold of our minds because we're believing in the power of our problems more than we believe in the power of God.

If we're going to love God with our minds, it is critical that we learn to believe God. He is above our circumstances and He has the final word in every area of our lives. He is working all things together for the good of those who love Him and are called according to His purpose (Romans 8:28). We don't have to figure out how we're going to overcome our problems because He has a plan, and His plan is good.

Throughout human history, God has displayed His power, love, and goodness through the stories of people dealing with terrible circumstances. Time and time again in Scripture, God stepped into what seemed to be hopeless situations and blessed His people. The elderly Abraham and Sara were far beyond childbearing years, but God blessed them with a son. Shadrach, Meshach, and Abednego were thrown into a fiery furnace as punishment for refusing to bow down to a man, but God preserved them in the flames. Daniel was thrown into a den of lions as the penalty for praying, but God closed the mouths of the lions. Couldn't God have given Abraham and Sara a son 50 years earlier? Changed the circumstances so that Shadrach, Meshach, and Abednego would never have had to spend even a second in the furnace? Kept Daniel from being

43

thrown into the lions' den in the first place? Yes, He is God; He can do anything. But for the sake of these godly people, for the sake of all those observing, for our sakes who read their stories in Scripture—for reasons beyond our understanding—God chose to work through their awful circumstances to display His glory.

God is always working His purposes, and we get a glimpse into God's ways in the story of the death of Lazarus. When Mary and Martha sent word to Jesus that their brother Lazarus was sick, Jesus purposefully delayed two days going to Bethany to visit Lazarus. Jesus allowed the circumstances to get worse. When it was time to go, Jesus told the disciples, *"Lazarus is dead. And I am glad for your sakes that I was not there, that you may believe"* (John 11:14–15). When Jesus and His disciples arrived, Mary and Martha were overcome with grief, the mourners were gathered, Lazarus had been in the tomb four days—by all reasoning of intellect, the matter was settled. Lazarus was dead. But then Jesus showed up and His words shattered the circumstances when He called Lazarus to rise up from the grave. The power of God was realized, and it all took place around a dead man's tomb.

God has the final word, not our enemies and not our circumstances. God can reveal His power in your life by defeating your circumstances. You can believe it.

Time to Think:

1. These are the bad circumstances in my life that I tend to dwell on:

2. When I think about the problem in my life of _____ _____, I have doubted that God is going to deliver a peaceful outcome because _____.

45

3. Do I ever think, *I know God can do anything, but* . . . ?

4. Am I rolling a problem around in my brain, trying to figure out how to fix it? What do I need to do with this problem as I love God with my mind?

What Were the Fishermen Thinking?

Luke 5:1–11

Peter and some other fishermen had been out all night fishing on the Lake of Gennesaret (the Sea of Galilee) and were now back to shore washing their nets when Jesus asked Peter to push his boat out a bit on the water. A mass of people had gathered, and Jesus would be better heard if He could back away from the crowd and speak from Peter's boat. Peter obeyed.

After the message, Jesus told Peter to venture deeper into the lake and lower his nets to catch fish. Seasoned fishermen knew that this made no sense. The best fishing on this lake was done at night, and Peter and the others were tired, perhaps even frustrated, because they had been up several hours with no fish to show for their all-night excursion on the lake. Besides, they had already washed their nets. The circumstances screamed that this was a fruitless exercise, so what would a very tired Peter do? He just had to say it—he had to let it be known that he and the others who were professional fishermen had already been at this endeavor for hours to no avail—but *"nevertheless"* (v. 5), whether out of respect for Jesus or to prove a point, Peter would do what Jesus said.

When Peter and the others pushed out deeper on the lake and let down the net, the volume of fish caught in the net was enough to make two boats nearly sink. It was such a powerful display of the authority of Christ that Peter fell down at Jesus' feet and cried out, *"Depart from me, for I am a sinful man, O Lord"* (v. 8). Surely Peter had been deeply convicted that his thoughts about Jesus and about the whole scene were horribly short-sided. After that event in their lives, Peter, James, and John *"forsook all and followed Him"* (v. 11).

These fishermen didn't necessarily need all of those fish. The story was never about fish. Perhaps when Peter and the others first pushed off into the deep, in their minds it was about fish. Perhaps they were wondering why Jesus would question their expertise in the trade of fishing. Perhaps they were thinking that Jesus would appreciate their compliance and hopefully stick to preaching from now on, letting them call the shots about fishing, after He had seen that He had put them to a lot of trouble for nothing. The circumstances seemed to say the problem was all about fish, but the work of Christ proves that it was never about fish at all, because Jesus chose to pour out such a supernatural blessing that the fishermen could not help but realize that He is Lord of all. If these men were going to be fishers of men, there would be dark days ahead filled with difficult circumstances, and in those days they would need to know that Jesus is Lord. One fishing excursion forever changed their thinking.

47

DAY 7: WHAT YOU HAVE TO KNOW, WHAT YOU DON'T HAVE TO KNOW

Thought: We struggle in our minds when we insist on knowing the answer to the question *why* for all our troubles and losses.

Challenge: Accept that God is control, and He can give you peace without having to answer all of your questions.

Knowing doesn't always make us feel better, but we think we need answers. If our spouse leaves us, we demand to know why. If our boss fires us, we want an explanation. It won't heal the marriage, nor will it give us the job back, but we think it will help us get peace about the loss.

But knowing doesn't bring peace. Answered questions only bring up more questions. *How long has my spouse felt this way? What would have happened if I had known about this earlier? Why didn't my co-workers tell me the boss was disappointed with me? Were the people in that office ever my true friends? Could I have done anything to stop this from happening?* The questions spiral to more questions, our minds formulate educated guesses, we toss it around over and over in our minds, and we try to make sense of it all.

What does that actually mean: "Trying to make sense of it all"? It typically means we won't let go of the problem and receive God's peace until we're satisfied. We're trying to figure out why it happened. We're trying to figure out who to blame. We're thinking about a chance to undo the situation and force things to go our way. Maybe we're trying to figure out how to turn the situation around so we can play the victim and everyone else involved will look like a villain. Maybe we eventually turn our thinking to how to exact revenge.

Never in Scripture did God reveal the fullness of *why* when one of His people suffered loss. Think about it: How could we possibly comprehend the fullness of His answers? In a world where billions of people are interacting every day, our minds couldn't comprehend the infinite layers of how one event in our lives affects countless other people in the present as well as the future. But the greater truth is this: that God demands that we trust Him. He is our Creator and Sustainer, and He never owes us an explanation. He does not have to justify Himself to us. God is God.

Think about how this truth brings freedom. When something bad happens to you—a door is shut—instead of jumping on the hamster wheel of round and round thinking about why, what happened, or who's at fault, you have the freedom to say, "God, I don't understand why You shut this door in my life, but it's enough to know that You love me and You're in control. I don't have to figure this out, because You've got it figured out." That's it. Peace. And it's a peace born of absolute faith in God's goodness.

Oh, how we struggle with questions in times of loss. And does God mind if we pose our questions to Him? Think about the plight of Job. He was a righteous man well known to God, but also well known to Satan. One day the evil accuser came to God with hate in his heart for Job, and he attacked Job's character. He claimed that Job only feared God because the Lord had prospered him. God had so much love and confidence in Job's faith that God allowed Job to be the man who would teach a lesson to Satan about the relationship between God and His people. In a swoop of destruction, God allowed Satan to take away Job's children and all of his wealth. Job's response was righteous; he worshipped God in the midst of the tragedy. *"Job did not sin nor charge God with wrong"* (Job 1:22). Job did not demand answers from God, and he rested in God's sovereignty.

But Satan continued to accuse Job, and God next allowed Satan to destroy Job's health. Job's wife did not have the moral character of Job, and she told her husband, *"'Do you still hold fast to your integrity? Curse God and die!'"* (2:9), but Job continued steadfastly to trust God, responding, *"'Shall we indeed accept good from God, and shall we not accept adversity'"* (2:10)? Even in the loss of his health, Job did not sin.

49

Next, Job's friends came along and tried to help Job figure out why he was going through all of this suffering. How could these mortals know? How could a man understand that God and Satan were battling over his righteousness? Job refused to go down that road of thinking.

Time passed, and Job knew God was in control, but Job finally went to a place of frustration. Have you ever hit a breaking point of faith and cried out to God in aggravation? Job declared that he did not understand and he wanted to know why God allowed this to happen to him. Can you relate? Job made it clear that He knew God was a righteous Judge and that all of His ways were beyond mankind's knowing, but Job was growing bitter. He was giving into the pangs of dissatisfaction and he demanded an explanation. He wanted God to justify His actions.

50

No, God did not strike Job dead. God listened to Job's long diatribe about his faithfulness and his afflictions, and God never interrupted. And in fact, when Job was done talking, God gave Job a lengthy response. Imagine the bravado Job must have been feeling to finally express in words all of the frustration toward God he was feeling in his heart, but then, try to capture the feeling of humility and smallness that surely consumed Job in the instant God spoke to Job out of a mighty whirlwind and said, *"Who is this who darkens counsel by words without knowledge? Now prepare yourself like a man; I will question you, and you shall answer Me'"* (38:2–3). Then God gave Job a glimpse of His glory. God reminded Job that He is the great I AM who existed before creation and who created all things. God is the One who knows when every animal is born in the wild. The earth and its elements obey Him. He exists and knows all things beyond the shadows of this earth. He is the Eternal One. He holds life and death. We are not to contend with God; He will not be corrected.

And Job's response? The same as ours, if we're wise. Job was humbled. He stood corrected. The awesomeness of God took over his mind and he once again remembered that it is a good thing that God alone knows all and is in control of our lives in the good times and bad. Job said, *"I lay my hand over my mouth'"* (40:4).

Are you questioning God? Are you driven in your mind to know *why* about the losses of life? Stop thinking about what you don't know, and start thinking about what you do know. You can strive and strain to know the answers of why, but you'll exhaust your mind over questions that God is not obligated to answer. But know this: *"The LORD is good; His mercy is everlasting, and His truth endures to all generations"* (Psalm 100:5). He holds your life in His hands. Love Him enough to rest in His peace.

Time to Think:

1. Is there any personal loss I have experienced that I still struggle to accept?

2. Is there an injustice in this world or a tragedy that a friend has faced that I am still questioning?

3. When I can't stop thinking about a disappointment or problem and I am trying to figure out why it happened, what is at the core of my desire to know?

_____ I am afraid it will happen again.

_____ I think God is punishing me.

_____ I am angry that I have been treated unfairly.

_____ I doubt that God loves me.

_____ I feel better when there's a person to blame.

_____ I want to control my life.

_____ I feel that when I'm doing my best to live righteously, God shouldn't allow bad things to happen.

_____ Other: _____

What Was Esther Thinking?

Esther 4

Her story began as an orphan being raised by her cousin Mordecai. Her life was turned upside down when the king of Persia's men gathered her up with scores of other pretty girls and carted them to the palace. There, she underwent beauty treatments with no promise whatsoever of what would happen to her if she was not picked by the king to be his bride. She had no way of really knowing what her life would be like if she *were* chosen to be queen. Much of the details of her life had been done to her, and were not of her doing.

Esther became queen and suddenly things began to change. She had the privileges of royalty. God had shown favor to Esther. Then out of nowhere, tragedy struck. Her people needed her to go before the king and plead on their behalf, and that very act could result in her execution. She was thrust into a position of danger, under the pressure of knowing that her people were counting on her.

Esther struggled with the decision. It was life or death for her but also for her people. Why did it have to be her? Why did it have to be now? She didn't ask for any of this responsibility, and once again in life, a plight was being thrust upon her. But like every other situation in life, Esther accepted that she would have to walk through this door with no explanation and no expectation, only trusting God.

It's not easy being queen. It's not easy following Christ. But God is faithful.

53

DAY 8: GOD WILL NOT BE RUSHED

Thought: No amount of pushing on our part will force God to fix our problems on our timetable.

Challenge: Let your mind rest from the turmoil of trying to force solutions.

Waiting is not one of my gifts. I have impatience sprinkled throughout my life history, often to my demise.

Childhood: I was a sneaky "bag-peeker" around Christmas and birthday time. The result was a few painful reminders on my posterior that peeking was not allowed. I had to learn that I'll get what I get when I get it. And did I learn the lesson? Well . . . I'm not a bag-peeker anymore, but I did accidently find my engagement ring in my boyfriend-now-husband's glove compartment because I was nosing around for a straw, compounded by the fact I had been dropping bomblike hints that I was getting impatient for a diamond. I ruined the surprise of the moment I had been waiting for all my life. Ruined.

Youth: OK, this is embarrassing, but I was a sneaky "boy-caller" whenever a boy I really liked hadn't called me as quickly as I thought he should. The result was a few painful humiliations when I either learned the hard way that there was a reason the boy hadn't called *or* when I scared off a very nice but shy boy who decided to move on because I was too pushy for his taste. I had to learn not to be aggressive and damage the natural progression of things. And did I learn that lesson? Well . . . my poor husband has graciously endured while I have very slowly learned not to hound him over yard projects, house repairs, decisions about vacation, and many other items when he's not doing things as quickly as I prefer that he would.

Adulthood: I have been a "solution-forcer." Once when I was in seminary and needed to earn some tuition money, I jumped at the first temp job that came along and was absolutely miserable for two weeks. I had to learn that I need to wait on God to provide the perfect resolution to my problem, not jump at any solution that comes within my arms' reach. And did I learn that lesson? Well . . .

The truth is that I'm still impatient to find out what good thing is just around the corner; I'm still prone to drive people nuts when I'm waiting on them to do something for me; and I still find myself occasionally dealing with the consequences when I settle for a quick solution instead of God's solution. I struggle to wait on God and perhaps you do too. We live in a fast-paced culture that trains us to expect instant results, speedy service, and on-demand solutions, but God doesn't operate under our mandates. We can't rush God.

55

The heart of the issue is self. We try to rush God when we're not getting what we want. We push matters when we're feeling uncomfortable. We don't like enduring pain, so we try to get relief. We don't like abstaining, so we rush gratification. We don't like the frustration of not knowing, so we push for answers. We don't like being under pressure, so we keep maneuvering until we're out from underneath the weight. We take control of the situation the best we can to force things to go our way. We might try to be very godly about this process, only fooling ourselves as we rationalize our decisions. We pray before we act, but we already have decided how we're going to act before we pray. We struggle with the feelings of panic and we doubt ourselves at every turn, but we push and we push and we pray to ask God to bless us as we act on our rush to judgment.

God invites us to *"rest in the LORD, and wait patiently for Him"* (Psalm 37:7). God once forced me to learn to rest and wait when He put me in a situation where I had no choice but to let Him bring a solution to my problem. When my husband and I thought we weren't able to have children, I had to come to the end of myself before I finally rested and waited on the Lord. First I chose to fret, then tried to figure out my medical problems, then tried to figure out what lesson God wanted me to learn first as if I could twist God's arm if I could get more spiritual, and finally—when there were no more websites to read, no more specialists to see, no more ideas I could present to God to explain why He was withholding this gift from me—I was forced to wait on God. I learned to sit still, read God's Word, and feel at rest in the Lord.

Everything clicked in my brain when I read this verse: *"Why are you cast down, O my soul? And why are you disquieted within me? Hope in God, for I shall yet praise Him for the help of His countenance"* (Psalm 42:5). God didn't want me to figure out my problems, He wanted me to trust Him enough to rest my hope in Him. God wanted me to desire Him more than I desired relief from my pain. God wanted me to appreciate His goodness in my life so much that I could praise Him with a smile even while I wasn't getting what I wanted.

In your most troubling times, God invites you to use your mind to hope in Him. Stop trying to cook up a plan to solve your problems. End the busyness of trying to make good things happen for yourself. Believe with your mind that in God's sovereignty, help is on the way; there's no need to try to rush God. Let your mind rest—God doesn't need you to figure it all out! He's got a plan.

Time to Think:

1. Do I rush people to give me answers or to do things for me? In those times, what is my priority?

2. Do I get impatient with God when I pray? How long should I be willing to wait on God's answer?

3. How often do I let go of my problems in my mind? When I finally (or temporarily) allow myself to let go, is it only because I'm gaining temporary satisfaction by eating a hot fudge sundae? Watching a movie? Partying with friends? Or is it because I'm resting in the Lord?

57

4. Do I try to help God solve my problems? What am I thinking during those times?

5. Do I try to help God solve other people's problems? What am I thinking during those times?

What Was Sarai Thinking?

Genesis 11:29–12:4; 16–18:15; 21:1–7

Abram was 75 when God promised to make him a great nation. Abram wasn't the only one thrilled with this great news. Sarai had been living with the shame of being barren in a culture that had no tolerance for wives who could not have children. What wonderful news! Sarai was going to know the joyous experience of carrying a child in her womb. The matter was settled, because God had promised her husband a child.

Time passed. How long before Sarai became discouraged? Six months? Two years? Five years? About 10 years after God made the promise, Sarai grew tired of waiting for this child, and she took matters into her own hands. She told Abram to have relations with her maidservant Hagar. Sarai was so desperate to have a child of her own that she was willing to receive God's promise of a child through the womb of another woman. Abram complied, and Hagar became with child.

Sarai had underestimated the personal anguish she would feel by getting just what she insisted on having, but by her own methods. Sarai looked at Hagar and saw a woman who had what she wanted—her husband's child in her womb—and she could not bear realizing that she had only herself to blame. God had made a promise, God's nature was to always be truthful, yet she had gotten impatient, desperate, and acted rashly. What a mess. She had ruined her relationship with Hagar, damaged her relationship with Abram, and done a horrible injustice to this child that would be born through Hagar. Such impatience led to this troubling act of faithlessness. Was all now lost? Nine months later, Hagar's baby was born. Sarai would watch this child grow for 13 years and wonder what kind of damage she had done to God's perfect plan.

When Abram was 99, God spoke to him again. God changed his name to Abraham and Sarai's to Sarah, and promised that she would have a son and be the mother of nations. One year later, Sarah gave birth to her son, Isaac, 25 years after God first made the promise. On the other side of a 25-year wait, Sarah said, *"God has made me laugh"* (21:6). What sweet perspective! Sarah learned that God could not be rushed, and when He fulfills His promises, His gifts are always worth the wait.

DAY 9: CHOOSING TO GLORIFY GOD

Thought: Praising God is a choice Christians make because of what we know about God, not because of what we're experiencing in the moment.

Challenge: Use your mind to dwell on God's goodness and faithfulness, and praise God at all times and in all things.

Think about what you would like for God to find you doing when Jesus returns. I would be thrilled beyond measure for God to split the skies wide open while I'm on a missions trip. How blessed I would be for God to find me sharing the Scriptures with my children at that moment described as the twinkling of an eye. If I would be sharing a message at a women's event, worshipping Him in song, serving in my church, or even doing something like vacuuming the carpet or folding laundry for my family, I would be so grateful to God. But if He should find me

59

gossiping with a friend or losing my temper at that appointed time, oh how ashamed I would be!

Imagine this scene: Paul and Silas are in prison. We don't know exactly what the prison was like, but judging from typical standards of the ancient world, it's not a stretch to imagine darkness, vermin, and stench. Paul and Silas had their feet in stocks, and they'd not been able to stretch their legs for hours by now. But the pain of muscle strain was not their greatest concern, because they had fresh wounds from a brutal beating on their bare backs that left them with bloody stripes. Their punishment was public, and their treatment unfair.

But God was about to intervene for these two men of faith. God caused an earthquake so great that every prison door was opened and every chain loosed. Praise God! He had looked upon Paul and Silas in their time of need and set them free. And when God showed up in the lives of these two men in prison, what did He find them doing? Much to their credit, God didn't find two men with scowls of anger upon their faces. God didn't hear words of complaint or worry. When God looked upon the two men He was about to set free, He saw Paul and Silas, bruised and weary, but fully focused on bringing glory to God. When God showed up, He found them praying and singing hymns to God.

What will God find you doing when He shows up to intervene on your behalf? When God answers your prayer, solves your problem, steps in to be your shield, delivers you from your enemies, provides for your need—at that moment, what will He find that you have on your mind? Will He find you bringing glory to His name in the midst of your troubles, or will He find your mind occupied with other things?

God challenges us to believe that He is as good as His word. *"Without faith it is impossible to please Him, for he who comes to God must believe that He is, and that He is a rewarder of those who diligently seek Him"* (Hebrews 11:6). Faith knows that God is going to show up. Faith is convinced that God will make a way where there is no way. Faith celebrates before the battle is over, because faith knows that God has already declared the outcome. Faith sings songs of praise in the night while shackled to a prison wall, because faith knows that no matter what, God is worthy of the glory due His name.

Glorifying God is a choice we make. We can glorify God in response to His intervention in our lives, and these victory songs honor Him. We can also glorify God before His intervention because we're responding not to our circumstances, but to His greatness. He is worthy that we might at all times, in all circumstances, and in every place, love Him with our minds so much that we cannot help but bring glory to His name.

61

Time to Think:

1 Do I commit time to think about God's glory every day?

2. When am I most aware of God's glory?

3. What best describes my "song" when I'm dealing with a problem?

_____ I sing a whiny song that's all about me and how much I'm hurting.

_____ I repeat a chorus of "it's not fair" to anyone who will listen.

_____ I can't sing. I shut down and try not to think about anyone or anything.

_____ I sing about God's glory because He is my Rock and I want to praise Him.

4. If someone near me had to describe my attitude toward personal suffering, what would he or she say?

5. Do I praise God daily?

What Were the Shepherds Thinking?

Luke 2:8–20

It had started out just like any other night. The same sheep, the same fields, the same men to guard the flock, resting under the same starry sky, but then God stepped into their ordinary night. Angels appeared to announce the glory of God! The Messiah was born. A Savior. The Christ Child. God's Son had arrived to earth in the form of a tiny babe, and they would find Him lying in a . . . did the angel really say that He was lying in a *manger*?

They had seen an angel. They had heard His message. They had experienced sheer bliss in their ears as an angelic host praised God in unison from the heavens above: *"Glory to God in the highest, and on earth peace, goodwill toward men"* (v. 14)! And now they would go and see this thing that the angel had spoken. A crowd of mangy shepherds traipsed through the night in search of this Baby, and they found that God's message was true. They met the King of kings in the manger. Their eyes had seen the glory of God.

As these shepherds returned to the fields to make their beds among the livestock, in many ways their lives had not changed. If a shepherd had begun his night with an ailing back or a toothache, he went to bed that night with an ailing back or a toothache. If a shepherd had started his evening knowing that he had a broken relationship with his wife, he left the manger scene still having that same trouble had home. In one sense, their lives had not changed. But in a different and very real sense, in the sense that matters for all of eternity, everything had completely changed. The shepherds had seen the long-awaited Savior, and God had spoken this great revelation very

63

specifically to them. The angels declared *"glory to God in the highest'"* as they announced the great news to the shepherds, and then it was the shepherds' turn to glorify and praise God as they returned to the fields. Their circumstances had not changed, but their lives were forever changed because they had met Jesus, and they could not help but bring glory to God.

The shepherds had been the first to arrive to worship Him, and yet when they left they were still lowly, humble men. As you draw near to Jesus Christ, you may also find that your circumstances remain the same. But like the shepherds, realize that when you come to the Savior, everything changes. You are changed. Those who draw near to Christ and look full into His face will not be able to help but go their way bringing glory to God in the highest.

DAY 10: LIVE FORGIVEN

Thought: When we confess our sins, God is faithful to forgive and forget our trespasses.

Challenge: Believe that God has forgiven you and let go of the shame.

Two phone calls. All I was asking for was two phone calls. My children know that when I'm on the phone they're supposed to step away to chat, or just be quiet. The first phone call was for business, and I was utterly humiliated as my children fussed with one another loudly in the background while I talked on the phone. After phone call one, I dealt out strong warnings for everyone to *hush!* The next call was to a dear friend, but nonetheless, I was still mortified that she could hear my children fussing in the background. By the time I hung up with my friend, I was livid.

Wow, was I ever getting my children up one side and down the other. I was hot, and they were going to feel the wrath of Mom. A good two minutes into the tongue-lashing I happened to gaze down at my lap, where my cell phone didn't look the way I had hoped; it wasn't sitting idle, as in fact I had accidently bumped the redial button. My friend had heard every word. I was horrified.

My friend—my sweet, godly friend—said, "Kimberly, it's OK. I remember those days, and I could tell you were frustrated. I was just praying for you, that God would give you patience with your children and that your children would behave better for the rest of the day."

As we hung up, my mind raced. *Will she always think less of me because she heard me fussing at my children in anger? And exactly what did I say? How bad did I sound? Maybe it was really bad, I can't remember . . . and am I a terrible mom? Maybe I am. I'm so ashamed of myself!*

I prayed and ask the Lord to forgive me for losing my patience with my children, and for all harm done with my words. I emailed my friend to explain the situation and asked her for forgiveness, but the relief I received from talking with her was only temporary. My guilt and shame were holding my thoughts hostage. I fretted about the incident for the rest of the day. I fought the thoughts, I told myself to let it go, but they kept resurfacing. I kicked myself over, and over, and over.

I couldn't stand myself any longer, and I finally found healing relief when I pulled aside to have a long talk with my heavenly Father. I needed Him to forgive me, and I believed that He had faithfully done that very thing as soon as I had asked for it, but now I needed to fully receive that forgiveness. I also needed God to remind me that I am human, I am still going to battle my sinful nature and sometimes lose, and that His forgiveness is complete.

The promise of 1 John 1:9 is a promise that brings great relief: *"If we confess our sins, He is faithful and just to forgive us our sins and to cleanse us from all unrighteousness."* The simplicity of God's promise is beautiful. Two things happen when we ask God's forgiveness: He forgives us, and He cleanses us from *all* that makes us wrong; He makes us right. He takes our crookedness and makes it straight. He takes our stains and removes them completely. He takes our scarlet letter and He replaces it with His mark of purity. When Christ enters our lives, we are absolutely set free from the shame of our sin. Forgiveness from God is deep, thorough, and complete.

66

Forgiveness is God's gift to us, and Jesus paid a high price to give us this gift. Have you ever watched someone open a gift you've given her, hoping to see the excited look on her face when she first lays eyes on the gift? Now think about how you respond to the gift of God's forgiveness. His gift of forgiveness makes you *"whiter than snow"* (Psalm 51:7). Are you relishing in the beauty of His gift of cleansing, or are you carrying around the shame of past stains? *"As far as the east is from the west, so far has He removed our transgressions from us"* (Psalm 103:12). He has purged your sin from your heart and His mind, but do you dwell on your sins and keep the shame in your mind?

When God forgives you, embrace the gift! Let go of your sin and guilt—it's not yours anymore. God's people are the ideal spokesmen to extol the power of God's forgiveness, but our message will only be effective when we can walk through this world like we're forgiven. And for that, we've got to believe that we're forgiven.

But do you deserve to feel so free? When your sin is ugly, or you've hurt others, or you know you've let God down, you may feel obligated to hold on to your guilt. You realize you deserve punishment, right? And in fact, as you've mulled this over in your mind, you're right. You deserve punishment. In fact, what you deserve is what every person on the face of the earth deserves, and that is the ultimate punishment—eternal separation from God (Romans 3:23; 6:23). But that is exactly why Jesus came. He took all of the punishment that you deserve when He suffered and died for you on the Cross. This is His gift, and if you've invited Christ to be your Savior and Lord, God would have you enjoy the fullness of His gift. *"If the Son makes you free, you shall be free indeed"* (John 8:36).

Reject the shame. Refuse to replay the stories of your sin over and over in your mind. When you feel guilt and shame popping up in your thoughts today, immediately tell God how grateful you are for His forgiveness. Then take a deep breath and smile. Be fully convinced that you are forgiven.

Time to Think:

1. Is there a shameful incident that I keep replaying in my mind? When I think about it, what particular part of the story do I dwell on?

2. Why do I think about this event so often?

3. This is what I want to say to God about His gift of forgiveness for this incident and for all of my sin:

4. Is there any incident in my past that was shameful because of what someone did to me? Who carries the burden of that sin before God?

What Was David Thinking?

2 Samuel 12:1–23

Oh, how the mighty had fallen. The great King David had lusted after another man's wife, committed adultery with her, impregnated her, attempted to deceive her husband, then had her husband killed. The king of Israel who was both a military leader and a spiritual beacon now had to face his own sin, and what a nasty dark blot it was. The humiliation was only going to spread, because David's sin would not be kept secret; God was going to reveal it.

The prophet Nathan confronted David, and David confessed His sin: *"I have sinned against the LORD"* (2 Samuel 12:13). God forgave David when he repented, but consequences would follow; the child that the woman Bathsheba would bare was going to die.

When the child became ill, David fasted and lay prostrate on the ground for seven days. On the seventh day, the child died. And David? The king got off the ground, washed and anointed himself, and went to the temple to worship. David had prayed to the Lord with hope that God might change His mind about the child, but now that the boy was dead, David was ready to move forward in his walk with God. He had made peace with his Creator, and he had made peace with the consequences of his sin. God had forgiven David, and now he must rise up and be a godly man once again. His nation needed him, his family needed him, and God was not done using David for His glory.

David still had much to do for the Lord, and you do as well. Repent, then think forward.

69

What Happens in the Secret Place

chapter three:

Both the inward thought and the heart of man are deep.

—Psalm 64:6—

The mind is a deep cavern. We share our thoughts with others from time to time, but even then we tend to craft our words to package our thoughts as we prefer for them to be received. Powerful thoughts are being formed in those caverns, so deep and hidden away that we often fail to appreciate their depth. Let's traverse to the recesses of the cavern with God and allow Him to shine a bright light on the truth of what is happening in the secret place that is our mind.

71

DAY 11: CONSIDERING YOUR WAYS

Thought: We need to know if we're fooling ourselves.

Challenge: Examine your decision making for signs of self-deception, and let God reveal the truth.

The Israelite people were facing ruination. An official document had been sealed by the king, and on a particular day of the calendar, their killing season had been declared. But they had an ace in the hole. The queen of the land was one of them. When Mordecai sent word to Queen Esther that her people were in danger of annihilation, he fully expected her to approach the king to intervene on her people's behalf. But when the news reached Esther, her first reaction was to back up and think. She considered the situation from her own perspective and how this situation could affect her personally if she spoke to the king. "It's not that easy," she replied to Mordecai.

Listen to Mordecai's retort to Esther: *"Think not with thyself that thou shalt escape in the king's house, more than all the Jews"* (Esther 4:13 KJV). Think not with thyself. Don't entertain this kind of thought-conversation between you and yourself. The NKJV translates the phrase as *"Do not think in your heart."* Mordecai knew that Esther's mind was racing back and forth, turning the decision over and over in her mind, playing the "what if" game. Was she contemplating how she could possibly manage to avoid putting herself in danger yet still come out smelling like a rose? Mordecai knew Esther all too well; after all, he was the man who had raised her. Mordecai was telling Esther, *don't fool yourself.*

It's the grand ruse. Women convene to sit around tables sipping drinks and laughing loudly with plastered grins, trying to convince themselves that all is well, though their families are falling apart at home. Men in suits flash confident smiles to their partners around the board table, hoping confidence on the outside will somehow breed confidence on the inside. People choose to eat, drink, and be merry with as much gusto as they can muster, hoping to ignore that their worlds are crumbling. The trickiest deception to pull off is when we manage to fool even ourselves.

On day 5, we unveiled the reality that every person spends a lot of time each day talking with himself. Throughout the day, we check in with ourselves: *Am I about to get myself fired, or am I justified to use this tone of voice at work? Since her boyfriend keeps stealing glances at me, shouldn't I keep stealing glances at him? Am I obligated to hand back to the cashier the extra five she gave me?* The risk we run is that we are fully capable of talking ourselves into all sorts of sin, justifying our actions, and convincing ourselves that what we know in our core to be wrong is somehow morphing into something that is right. With practice, we can get really good at lying to ourselves.

These kinds of mind games can lead to what Paul called a seared conscience (1 Timothy 4:2). We hedge the truth; we hesitate to do what's best if we think we can sneak by with what's simply OK, if it helps our cause. And because of the self-deception, we then cannot figure out why we're faltering spiritually. Why isn't God blessing? Why can't we hear the voice of God? Why are we struggling to know God's will?

God has said, *"Consider your ways"* (Haggai 1:5). Take a careful look at your ways. How do you talk to people? How do you respond to temptations where it appears you could cut a corner and no one would know? When you sense God telling you to make a personal sacrifice of your money or time but you really don't want to do it, do you deny your flesh and make the sacrifice or do you explain to yourself that it's best for you and fine with God to postpone the sacrifice? When you can honestly evaluate your ways, you're in a much better position to honestly evaluate the decisions you're making that led to those ways, and discern from God if you're fooling yourself in any area of your thought life. Ways trace back to decisions, decisions trace back to thoughts, and thoughts trace back to how much or little of our minds we have fully surrendered to the lordship of Jesus Christ.

Time to Think:

1. The last time I was tempted to do something wrong, what was it? How did I talk myself into doing it?

2. Is there any decision I've made lately that I wouldn't want revealed to other people? Why don't I feel comfortable telling it openly?

3. When I read a command in the Bible or hear a sermon with a teaching that I really don't want to have to follow, what are usually my inward thoughts?

What Was Cain Thinking?

Genesis 4:1–8

Nobody really knows what Cain was thinking, but we could imagine. What Cain had prepared as a sacrifice for the Lord was unacceptable, and he was busted. We've all been in that place of feeling embarrassed about our shortcomings, and we could guess what any person in his position might be tempted to think:

- *This is completely unfair. I did the best with what I had to offer.*
- *This is the way God made me. He knows I'm not a hunter. Surely God wouldn't have wanted me to bring an animal sacrifice, not me of all people, so I just don't get it; this should have been good enough.*
- *Actually, I may have just misinterpreted what God said. Everything's fine.*
- *What I offered to God was completely reasonable. Anyone who disagrees is legalistic and judgmental.*
- *When my life circumstances get better, my sacrifice will get better. I can't help it right now.*
- *I'm' not being punished for any mistake I've made. Satan is just attacking me. I'm human, so I'm going to have these kinds of trials from time to time. This is an opportunity for me to grow stronger as I suffer through this, that's all. But I hate that this is happening to me.*
- *Abel is so self-righteous. He is no better than me. He just does things like this to appear better than me.*
- *At least my heart was in the right place.*

75

- *I was just tired from working so hard. Maybe if I explain it to God in this way, it will seem that I really didn't do anything wrong and I won't have to feel guilty.*
- *I don't have time for this. I'm angry, and someone is going to make this right for me.*
- *I do all of this for God, and what happens? I end up completely humiliated. Why do I even try?*
- *I know what everyone's thinking about me because my offering wasn't accepted. They're bigger sinners than me for thinking it.*
- *I've got to do damage control, and quickly. I'll tell everybody who knows about this that God and I talked, and . . .*

Actually, the place Cain's mind chose to go was anger, and he wasn't trying to hide it; the fury was written all over his face. God explained the situation to Cain in very simple terms: when we do what is right, we stand acceptable before God, and when we do poorly, sin is present. Sin is crouching, desiring to pounce, and we must fight those sinful thoughts from entering our minds and driving us to a sinful reaction.

God intervened in Cain's anger, giving him the opportunity to stop and think, to correct his attitude and learn from the experience, but Cain would not change his mind. Cain stubbornly insisted on deluding himself about his guilt before God. He would not consider his ways. Instead, Cain indulged the anger, embraced the sin, and his angry thoughts led to violent ways. Cain killed his brother.

Consider your ways and admit any thoughts you're entertaining that are nothing more than self-delusion. Let God change your mind before those self-deceiving thoughts give way to actions, because sin is crouching at the door.

DAY 12: CONVINCED AND DETERMINED

Thought: Doing the right thing takes mental strength.

Challenge: Do what you know is right.

Everyone makes moral decisions on a daily basis, though not everyone is aware of the morality of his or her choices. On the surface, the decision may appear to be a choice of what's best for the business or what's going to keep peace in the family, but behind daily decisions are the moral beliefs that give shape to our thoughts.

Adam and Eve were the first two people, and God had given them the gift of choice. In the garden, Eve wasn't deciding what to eat for breakfast; she was looking at the fruit from the Tree of the Knowledge of Good and Evil and deciding who was telling the truth, God or the serpent. Eve made judgments about the fruit, considering its appearance and what she believed the fruit would do for her. She wasn't convinced that there would indeed be consequences from eating the fruit, as God had said. She didn't do what she knew to be right, and she ate the fruit. The consequences were devastating.

When it comes to making moral decisions, we sometimes struggle to know what's right. What a sad commentary of mankind that so many people in the world float through life and never find an anchor. They never tether themselves to a Solid Rock, to give them clarity of mind and a center for moral judgments. Those who "go with the flow" or "live and let live" are like a ship with no sail, blown about by the storms of life and are often dashed against the rocks to their destruction. But for those who have tethered themselves to Jesus Christ, we have sure footing on His truths, and our moral center is

77

whatever God says is right and wrong. Simple. When we find ourselves saying, "The world has gotten so complicated," we're just parroting the propaganda machines of the world that are chipping away at our moral foundation, trying to get us to crumble over moral issues. The world is complicated, but it has always been complicated. There has always been good versus evil. There has always been a strong wave of the majority who do not love God and do not like the morality of God. And Satan has always been deceptive, twisting the truth and trying to get us to buy into his version of the truth.

We can know what's right. The first step in making a moral decision is deciding that we believe God. When we submit that God defines right from wrong, suddenly life becomes less complicated. We do what we know is right, and we trust that the results for ourselves and for those around us will be according to God's will. We don't have to figure everything out, and we don't have to plot a course to make all of the dominoes line up the way we want them to fall. God is sovereign; we do what He says, and we leave the rest to Him.

And what about those areas where we struggle with gray? When a moral issue seems gray, we must check to see if the truth is plainly spelled out in God's Word, and we're just avoiding the truth because we're hoping for another option. But certainly, even the early Christians had their share of struggles over knowing how best to exercise their freedom in Christ. Paul exhorted Christians, *"Let each be fully convinced in his own mind"* (Romans 14:5). Before we place our stamp of approval on an activity that once seemed gray, we must be absolutely certain that God is giving us permission to move forward.

But once we're convinced of what is right, the second element of a moral decision is doing what we know to be right. I've always been in awe at the Prophet Daniel's ability to know what is right, and then to do it. His decision making was solid throughout his career, which was no small feat for a man who served in leadership as a captive in a land of men who had no fear of God. The nation's leadership was often quite anti-God, yet Daniel refused to be a product of his environment. His name means "God judges me" and he never seemed to forget his namesake. Perhaps one of the keys to Daniel's success was a decision he made early on as a young man in captivity in Babylon: *"Daniel purposed in his heart that he would not defile himself"* (Daniel 1:8). He was determined that He would do what was right in the sight of God.

Convinced and determined. Be convinced in your mind that God defines right from wrong, then be determined to do what is right. How do you love God with your mind when you're making moral decisions? You stay true to what you know is right. No plotting. No scheming. These are two activities of the mind that bring no glory to God. Check yourself against any sentence that begins like this: "Yeah, but I was just trying to..." No complicated schemes to skirt around the moral edge; either we decide to do what God says is right to please Him, or we decide to do what we prefer and please ourselves. Be convinced and be determined.

79

Time to Think:

1. What is the last moral decision that I made? What ideas did I roll around in my mind as I made that decision?

2. When I am tempted to do something that I know is wrong, I tend to:
   _____ Scheme a way not to get caught.
   _____ Try to twist the situation around to make it seem like what is wrong is actually right.
   _____ Fight the thoughts of temptation and tell myself that I know what is right.
   _____ Admit to God that I'm tempted, so I'll remember that I'm accountable to Him.

3. Are there any social issues that I struggle with because the Bible teaches that an activity or lifestyle is wrong, but I can see the logic of those who feel differently about the issue? What are those logic points? (Write them down.) How would God respond to those logic points? (Prayerfully write a response.)

What Was Pharaoh Thinking?

Exodus 8:1–15

Pharaoh had a revolting problem. He had refused to release the Israelite people, God's chosen people, from their bondage. He had taken them into captivity, and it seemed only right that these people belonged to him. *My land, my military might, my slaves.* Moses said otherwise. Moses said that God wanted His people released, and God was ready to do something about it if Pharaoh wanted to play hardball. Pharaoh had no respect for the power and authority of God. Pharaoh was more than happy to say, "Game on."

Pharaoh became overwhelmed with God's second plague: frogs. They were everywhere and in everything. Consider the sound of thousands of frogs croaking from across the land, across your yard, and in unison with the frogs that were under your feet, on your bed, and in your lap. I can only imagine how the sights and sounds of that many frogs would make a person feel pushed to the edge of sanity.

Pharaoh couldn't take it, and he called for Moses and Aaron to talk to God. Pharaoh was ready to let the Israelites sacrifice to their God. Moses cried out to God, and the Lord was faithful; He caused all of the frogs to die. Now imagine this scene: masses upon masses of frogs now lay dead across the land, and *"the land stank"* (v. 14). Pharaoh looked across the landscape and saw the people raking up piles of dead frogs, and with the smell of dead frogs still in his nostrils—with a sense of relief that the crisis had passed—Pharaoh decided to keep the Israelites in captivity.

Pharaoh knew what God wanted, He knew what God was capable of, but he simply didn't respect God. Pharaoh wanted

81

God's blessings, or to say the least he didn't want God's curses, but he didn't want God. Pharaoh wasn't convinced that God was right, and he was fiercely determined to run his kingdom his own way, to please himself. What is your fierce determination?

DAY 13: LIKE-MINDED WITH GOD'S PEOPLE

Thought: God desires for His people to be like-minded with one another.

Challenge: Yield your thinking to God's authority, and with humility be like-minded with fellow Christ followers.

82

You've heard the expression, "If looks could kill," but what if thoughts could kill? What if the malice we felt toward others could be balled up and catapulted in their direction for a direct blow to their hearts? Who would survive a day in this world? But God is calling His people to a higher way of thinking toward one another. To love God with our minds, we must use our minds to love God's people.

Our thoughts toward one another will either drive us away from one another in mistrust and disdain, or we'll become so unified that we can work together to accomplish anything according to God's will. Paul wrote, *"Now may the God of patience and comfort grant you to be like-minded toward one another, according to Christ Jesus, that you may with one mind and one mouth glorify the God and Father of our Lord Jesus Christ"* (Romans 15:5–6). We will fall short of God's purpose for our lives unless we learn to be like-minded with other believers. As Christians, we are a critical component of God's plan to bring the message of redemption to the world. We've got to work in unison if we're going to accomplish God's will. Only then can we tell of the glory of God with one great voice for the whole world to hear.

We are to be so interrelated with one another that we realize that we're family. We are to be so interconnected that we're functioning like one body with many body parts. And God desires that our relationships with one another be not just functional, but also relational. Working together for God's glory goes well beyond simply what we do, like robots working on an assembly line to create a finished product, but is more like a countless number of voices and instruments coming together to make beautiful music that brings glory to God.

Scripture has much to say about the way we are to think of one another:

83

- We are to think of one another with love. Jesus said, *"By this all will know that you are My disciples, if you have love for one another"* (John 13:35). Love is more than like. Love is more than tolerate. Love isn't just an emotion to be manipulated by circumstances. Love is patient and kind, and it isn't boastful, rude, or envious; it endures (1 Corinthians 13). Love isn't lip service, but it is expressed in actions that reveal our true affection for one another (1 John 3:18).

- We are to desire to be in unity and harmony. We are brothers and sisters in Christ. We are a family unified to bring glory to God. We are under the authority of Christ. God's Word instructs us to *"speak the same thing, and that there be no divisions among you, but that you be perfectly joined together in the same mind and in the same judgment"* (1 Corinthians 1:10). Fights break out among God's people when we have evil desires and we seek after those desires with pride and greed (James 4:1–6). The world is filled with many voices crying out for their own desires, but God's people are to be unified in our desire, that we might have a mind so unified that we can speak with one voice the message of God's glory.

- We are to think of others as valuable contributors to the body of Christ. We tend to be in love with our own opinions, but God teaches us a better way. *"In lowliness of mind let each esteem others better than himself"* (Philippians 2:3). Paul said it another way in his letter to the Romans: *"Do not be wise in your own opinion"* (Romans 12:16). Yield to the ideas of other Christians, and value what God is saying through them. Be willing to learn from God through others.

84

- We are to think of others as worthy of our servitude. *"If anyone desires to be first, he shall be last of all and servant of all"* (Mark 9:35). Servanthood is not just about getting down on our hands and knees and doing work. It's the mind-set of the servant that makes the work servanthood; otherwise, we're only piously showing off how low we can go for others to admire our good deeds. Note that God is not only calling us to serve, but to be so humble in our attitudes that we *"serve one another"* (Galatians 5:13).

It's much easier to love God, bow to the desire of God for the sake of unity with Him, esteem His wisdom far above our own, and think Him worthy of our servitude. But God requires us to express our love for Him by thinking these same things of His other children, those who are made in the image of God and who have been adopted into the family of God. Look deep into your mind and consider your thoughts toward other believers. Look past the façade of your politeness and general congeniality toward others, and examine your true thoughts toward other people. Are you loving God by loving others?

Time to Think:

1. As I interact with other Christians, I tend to:

   _____ Tell it like it is. I don't try to filter my words. What I say matches what I think.

   _____ Show people respect and kindness, but I confess that I'm sometimes faking it.

   _____ Other:

2. As I understand it, God wants me to be of the same mind with other believers because:

85

3. The person I'm struggling to be like-minded with is _____. On my part, God is telling me to change my mind about:

4. The next time I disagree with someone in the body of Christ, I'm going to acknowledge that my thoughts toward other Christians matters to God, and I am going to:

What Was Miriam Thinking?

Numbers 12

God works in mysterious ways. Moses was gone for so long, enjoying a peaceful existence with his family and friends, while we were languishing in cruel bondage, isolated from the outside world, never knowing the taste of freedom. I'm glad I was there to help get my baby brother into the arms of safety, even if it was so that he could live like a king as Pharaoh's daughter's child. I'm glad he returned to Egypt to usher me and our people to our promised land. But why must he get all the glory? Why must everyone look up to him alone? What about Aaron? What about me? Why can't Moses share a little bit of the glory? I've helped him, Aaron's helped him . . . it's time for him to share some of the spotlight.

Miriam was through with standing in Moses' shadow. She and Aaron had hatched a plan to turn the people away from Moses and toward themselves. They attacked Moses' character on the subject of his Ethiopian wife, and they planted a seed of doubt in the people's minds about Moses' leadership. God knew their thoughts, and He heard their words.

Perhaps Miriam was the mastermind behind the grand scheme, because only she received the punishment of leprosy and the resulting public humiliation of seven days' quarantine from the camp. What was she thinking when she created the scheme? It appears her thoughts were of envy, bitterness, and pride. What was she thinking during her seven days of isolation? Perhaps she reflected deeply upon her inner thoughts toward Moses, and came to grips with the hidden seeds of anger in her heart that had led to this humiliating display of her sinfulness.

What do you see when you look into your mind at the thoughts you have toward your brothers and sisters in Christ? What change of mind is God calling you to, before you would suffer the consequences of ill intensions toward your brother?

DAY 14: WHEN YOU CHOOSE TO LET GO

Thought: Unforgiveness enslaves our minds to the power of anger.

Challenge: Choose to let go of past hurts by forgiving others, freeing your mind to focus on God.

I once did a season of women's revivals. Every revival weekend was an exciting worship experience as God drew women to the foot of the Cross, wrapped them in His love, and met their deepest needs. At one point in the revival, I would invite women to go into the corner of the sanctuary of their choice, based on a particular need. Some women went to the corner for women who felt God's calling in their lives and longed to know His will. Other women went to the altar to intercede for the nation. Others went to a corner of the sanctuary with other women who desired to be rid of a sinful habit. Always several women went to the corner of the sanctuary dedicated to those women who were ready to let go of unforgiveness.

Unforgiveness is one of the great hindrances to loving God with our minds. Its power of destruction is multifaceted:

• Unforgiveness is a mental distraction. To hold a grudge takes up shelf space in our gray matter. We have to retain the details of the memory of the wrong that was done to us in order to keep the wound fresh. We have to check ourselves to be certain that the fire stays kindled, so as not to relent on the full fury we feel that our oppressors deserve. We must also stay strong not to give in to fatigue, sentiment, or any other weakness that could sway us from the unforgiveness.

- Unforgiveness is a self-inflicting weapon. The more you lunge it toward others to injure them, you yourself receive multiple wounds. I once met with a woman who had finally chosen to forgive her attacker after 50 years of holding hostility toward him. Not merely the incident, but also her unforgiveness attached to the incident had sabotaged every relationship she had attempted in a half-century span. She realized she was a bitter person, and she had never been able to put her finger on the source of her negativity until she acknowledged her problem and forgave her attacker.

- Unforgiveness is bondage. We're trying to hold someone else hostage by locking him up in chains of unforgiveness, only to realize that what we've done is effectively chain ourselves to our assailant so that we also can't break free.

If you're serious about loving God with all your mind, it's time to forgive. God commands us to forgive just as we have been forgiven by Christ. However, unforgiveness won't give up without a fight. We're going to have to be mentally tough to cut through layers upon layers of unforgiveness. We're going to face wrong thoughts that will surface to our brains when we think about forgiving someone:

- *She needs to suffer longer.* We must turn that statement around to think, *I don't need to suffer any longer.* We exaggerate the pain we're inflicting on others if we think that our unforgiveness inflicts suffering to them in the same measure that it pains us. And the suffering for us is great, because our unforgiveness is sin. No matter how horribly wronged we've been, no matter how malicious the injury placed upon us, it is we who will suffer spiritually from unforgiveness because the unforgiveness creates a barrier between us and God. Jesus said, *"For if you forgive men their trespasses, your heavenly Father will also forgive you. But if you do not forgive men their trespasses, neither will your Father forgive your trespasses'"* (Matthew 6:14–15). That's simply too high a price to pay; we must end our suffering.

- *If I forgive him, I'm only letting him off the hook.* God is the righteous Judge. We will never determine the measure of punishment that others receive, no matter how long we prolong the unforgiveness. God can exact consequences that extend well beyond our punitive unforgiveness, and His judgments are sure. Forgiveness, then, takes a measure of faith that God will be a fair Judge in the matter as He deals with both the victim and the oppressor.

- *He's not even sorry; I don't have to forgive him.* As Jesus was being crucified, He was surrounded by those who had whipped Him and mocked Him, blasphemers, those who had cast lots for His garments, gawkers, and doubters, and Jesus said, *"Father, forgive them, for they do not know what they do'"* (Luke 23:34). We must also forgive as Christ forgave us (Colossians 3:13), willingly and freely, remembering that while we were yet sinners Christ demonstrated His love for us (Romans 5:8).

89

- *The anger is the only way I can cope with what he did to me.* No, with God's help you can forgive. You can turn off the reels of footage that run again and again in your mind, replaying the incident that hurt you deeply. You can get beyond coping and begin healing. You will be freed from the chains of the hurt when you choose to be freed from the chains of unforgiveness.

It's time to move on and let go. It's time to release the people who have wronged you from the chambers where you've kept them locked up in your mind. It's time to be obsessed in your thinking about God, and no longer obsessed in your thinking about the one who has hurt you. Let your mind be free to love.

Time to Think:

1. On a scale of 1 to 5, how easy is it for me to forgive? (1 is complete unforgiveness; 5 is quick to forgive.)

2. As I think carefully about the events of my life and how I've responded to the wrongs done to me, am I still holding anger, a grudge, or unforgiveness toward anyone:

From my childhood?

From my teen years?

From my early adult life?

From recent events?

3. The prophet Jonah was enraged when God forgave the Ninevites from their sins. He wanted them to suffer for all of the evil they had done. He wanted to see justice. Who is the person that I would like to see punished for their wrongdoings? As I read what God said to Jonah in Jonah 4:4, God is saying to me:

91

What Was Joseph Thinking?

Genesis 45:5–8; 50:19–21

What Joseph's brothers had done to him triggered a series of painful circumstances in his life. They were jealous of him, so they sold him into slavery. He was taken away from his father who adored him and the comforts of home. What's more, God had given the young Joseph a dream of greatness for his future, and the day he was sold into slavery would have appeared to have been the day that the dream died. Then things got worse. While serving as a slave, he was wronged again, this time by his master's wife who accused him of attempted rape, causing him to be thrown into prison. Then again, things got worse. He helped two servants of the king, and he had great hope that one of the servants would secure his release from prison, but the servant forgot him and left him to rot in prison.

But all the while, Joseph prospered. He was the head servant as a slave in the first stop of his journey. Then he was given great liberties and responsibilities even while in prison. Joseph didn't get bitter. He didn't obsess over the wrongs done to him, or bemoan his situation. He chose to flourish wherever God planted him, and this level of forgiveness and faith allowed Joseph to stand before his brothers and love them, exacting no revenge though it was completely within his power to do so. Whether serving as a slave, living as a prisoner, or making life-altering decisions as a ruler, Joseph lived freely above his circumstances because Joseph learned to let go. Have you?

92

DAY 15: ALL IN

Thought: God knows our every thought; He knows every square inch of our minds, both that which we openly share with Him and also the hidden places.

Challenge: Purposefully invite God to reign in every area of your mind.

When my husband and I bought the house where we now live, one of the key selling points was the unfinished basement. My husband had talked about wanting a man cave, and I had dreamed of designing it for him. Actually, I wanted it to be our cave, because I hoped to decorate the space around a common interest we have in all-things-sports from our college alma mater. For an entire year, I daydreamed, sketched, measured the floor space, and thumbed through magazines for the best ideas of making our sports den. Then the day came that I was finally able to purchase the paint and order the floor tile—everything orange and purple. For a moment, I took pause to think about what I was doing. I was about to decorate an entire level of my house, ceiling to floor tile, *in orange and purple.* I realized this move was a major commitment, and it was a point of no turning back. In good times and bad, in winning seasons and losing seasons, I was going to be residing in orange and purple. After only a moment of hesitation, I made my choice. I was all in.

So when the new football coach at Clemson University, Dabo Swinney, began his tenure with the slogan "All In," I knew exactly what he was talking about. Dabo was asking every fan, coach, and player to believe that the team can and will win, and he was asking for a commitment from everyone involved to give their all to the effort of making it happen. He was asking for the kind of

93

support that would bring a fan to paint her basement orange and purple, and my husband and I were already there. We're all in.

Football is fun and builds character, but even a football nut like me realizes that "all in" for your favorite team deserves a limited amount of commitment. God is calling us to the highest tier of surrender, being "all in" for God and His kingdom.

Imagine that your mind is sectioned off by walls and doors. How many rooms have you completely devoted to God? These are the rooms with doors that remain unlocked, open for inspection and redecoration at God's bidding. Maybe your "money" room is open to God; you have no secrets to hide about how much you tithe, your level of giving, and how you spend your money. When God says give, you give, no questions asked. Perhaps your "marriage" room has a door that's wide open. You desire God to permeate that space, and you've given your spouse and your marriage completely to the Lord. You love your spouse and keep your vows with joy, as unto the Lord.

Possibly your "missions" room is vibrant with color that reflects the diversity of all peoples, and the walls are jumping with the beat of the song of the nations; you love to spend time with God in this room, reminiscing over past missions trips and praying about the people you've met in foreign lands, but you politely usher God to the door and shut it behind Him when He starts talking about career missions; He's welcome to stay as long and as often as He would like in the missions room, and He can paint the walls in the colors of any flag, as long as He has the understanding that your surrender is for short-term trips only.

Then there's your "job" room. The door is open, though you feel uncomfortable about talking with God in this room because you're not really sure you want to hear what He might say. But in this room of stark white and dim lighting is a closet door, locked, and you keep possession of the key apart from

God. That one particular aspect of how you do your job is not up for discussion with God.

The rooms that are shut off from God might be your storage space for anger toward Him for not answering your prayers the way you wanted, or for piles of grudges that you hold toward your mother for being absent when you needed her most. Other rooms may be blocked off because you simply don't want to address them with God, like unpaid debts you would rather not pay or spiritual disciplines you don't want to engage. You may know what's in those rooms and have a label over every door, or you may find it too challenging to address those rooms and you've simply shut off a whole wing of rooms by turning out the lights and blocking the entrance.

Jesus said, *"Whoever desires to come after Me, let him deny himself, and take up his cross, and follow Me'"* (Mark 8:34). The call to live for Christ is a call to complete surrender. And at times Jesus chose to be specific about what full surrender means. For instance, Jesus also said that you cannot be His disciple if you put loved ones, including yourself, before Him (Luke 14:26); there can be no rooms blocked off for what you will not do because you feel that the cost to your relationships with your family and loved ones is too great. Our careers, our health, our finances—even our relationships—belong to Him.

Begin walking through the halls of your mind. Inspect each room. Rejoice with God over rooms that are already open, and dare to begin unlocking doors of the hidden spaces. Be honest with yourself and speak the truth to God. He already knows what's behind every door, but you are the one who is blessed and healed when you open the door and invite God to reign in every space of your mind. You'll be "all in" for the Lord when you know that He is "all in" every thought, every decision— every aspect of your mind.

95

Time to Think:

1. Am I currently living fully surrendered to God? Has my level of surrender changed through the years?

2. As I look at the rooms of my mind, how transparent am I before God?

   My finances:
   _____ This matter is completely laid bare before the Lord.
   _____ I am trying to keep some control for myself.
   _____ I have not been able to surrender this area of my life to God.

   My love relationship(s):
   _____ This matter is completely laid bare before the Lord.
   _____ I am trying to keep some control for myself.
   _____ I have not been able to surrender this area of my life to God.

   My past:
   _____ This matter is completely laid bare before the Lord.
   _____ I am trying to keep some control for myself.
   _____ I have not been able to surrender this area of my life to God.

   My recreation/entertainment:
   _____ This matter is completely laid bare before the Lord.
   _____ I am trying to keep some control for myself.
   _____ I have not been able to surrender this area of my life to God.

My family:

_____ This matter is completely laid bare before the Lord.

_____ I am trying to keep some control for myself.

_____ I have not been able to surrender this area of my life to God.

My interactions with people I don't like:

_____ This matter is completely laid bare before the Lord.

_____ I am trying to keep some control for myself.

_____ I have not been able to surrender this area of my life to God.

97

3. Because of my desire to love God with every part of my thinking, I want to begin talking with God about:

What Was the Young Man Thinking?

Matthew 19:16–22; Mark 10:17–22; Luke 18:18–23

You can't fool God. The rich young ruler sought out the Lord because he wanted what money can't buy: He wanted eternal life. Jesus had no trouble seeing through the young man's thoughts, and He knew his eagerness, yet Jesus also knew about the one particular room of his mind that the young man had shut away from God. Jesus loved him, and He pointed out this aspect of the young man's life that would be his hardest to surrender to God. Jesus told the rich young ruler to surrender his wealth.

98

The young man made a decision to walk away from Jesus. Complete surrender wasn't his choice, because his mind was made up that the cost was too great. He esteemed his wealth above the riches of eternal life.

As you hear the call of Jesus to surrender all, how do you esteem the value of what's hiding behind the locked doors of your mind?

chapter four
Decisions, Decisions

There are many plans in a man's heart,
Nevertheless the Lord's counsel—that will stand.
—Proverbs 19:21—

We've all got our decisions to make. Life is a series of decisions. Sometimes we feel like we don't have a choice in a matter, and other times we feel like we're drowning in a sea of options. We need God to take the reins of our mind and guide us to make decisions that will honor Him. We don't want to fight Him; we want to join Him. We don't want to tell Him what we will do, but we desperately need Him to tell us what we should do. A mind that loves God is actively seeking to know His will.

DAY 16: DISCERNING GOD'S WILL

Thought: Followers of Christ want to know God's will in order to fulfill God's will.

Challenge: Ask the right questions in your quest to discern God's will.

We're filled with questions for God, but the question that leaves us straining to be patient for answers is the question of God's will for our lives. We want yes and no answers to our questions, we want detailed instructions—we'd actually prefer it if God would draw us a map! The more we realize the complexities of life and the ripple effects of every decision we make, the more we yearn to get it right as we step out each day to fulfill God's great purpose for us. We need to hear from God, and we need Him to guide our thinking.

Are you currently wrestling with decisions? Consider the questions you've asked God in your quest to know His will.

- **Do you ask God for answers or explanations?** Do we trust God? Is it enough for us to know that God is omniscient, omnipotent, and omnipresent, and thus far more qualified to make decisions than we are, or must He justify Himself to us? When God begins to guide our thinking and reveals His will to us, we have a choice. Option one is to trust Him and obey. Or, we can refuse to acknowledge that we've heard from God, act like the decision is still up in the air, and procrastinate until we think God's answer makes sense in our minds.

- **Do you frame your questions from the proper perspective?** All that we do should bring glory to God. Our earthly citizenship may offer us the right to life, liberty, and the pursuit of happiness, but our citizenship in heaven has no such declaration. We may suffer, we may lose, we may be put to shame, we may experience hardship, we may miss out on comfort or pleasure, we may do things that cause our loved ones to miss out on comfort or pleasure, we may walk into danger, we may traverse the valley of the shadow of death— all for the glory of God.

100

With this perspective, the only appropriate question in seeking God's will is completely centered on the way we can best bring honor and glory to God, regardless of the cost to us. We take thoughts of self out of the equation. We even somewhat backseat our worries about how our decisions will affect others, since ultimately we serve God alone, and He loves others in greater capacity than we could ever begin to love. We completely focus on God. The question, "God, can I afford to do this?" is replaced with "God, will this bring glory to Your name?" Instead of asking, "God, will this get me further in my career?" we ask, "God, are you calling me to do this so that I might honor You?" Instead of "what is best for me" questions, we ask "what is best for God's kingdom" questions.

101

- **Do your questions to God match the questions you're asking yourself?** We can be spiritually minded as we voice our questions to God, but what we mull over all day long in our private thoughts are powerful to influence our decision-making process. We may come to God to ask, "Lord, do You want me to go on this missions trip?" and then spend the rest of the afternoon asking ourselves, "Can my children manage without me for a week?" The questions we're asking ourselves lead us to make an educated guess to the answers, and what will we do if our educated guess is in direct opposition to the answer God gives? It's then that we find ourselves saying, "I think God is calling me to do this, but . . . ", and we finish that sentence based on the answers we have delivered for ourselves. We have created our own conflict, because we asked a question of God and separately consulted ourselves.

- **Do you ask questions that you're willing to have answered?** I joke with my husband that it's no fair asking me what restaurant I want to go to if you're going to reject every choice that I suggest! There's no need to enter the throne room of God with a question if we're not willing to accept the answer.

It's no small thing to seek the mind of Christ. Our Savior was completely yielded to the will of the Father, even unto death on the Cross. It was not the decision His friends or His mother would have made for Him. It was not a choice that His flesh (that which made Him fully man) agreed with, either. We see Jesus agonizing over the weight of the Cross as He prayed to His Father in the Garden of Gethsemane. Yet as we see Jesus walking through the hours that followed, when He was arrested in the garden up until the moment when He uttered, "It is finished," on the Cross, we see our Lord completely resolved to fulfill the will of the Father. We, too, can be resolved to press forward even in the midst of difficulty when we know we're fulfilling the will of God.

How can you be sure that you know? When can you be satisfied that you've heard from God? The truth of the matter is that we likely know the answer before we get to a place of peace, where we're finally willing to admit it. Saying out loud that we have an answer makes the decision feel final, and we delay saying anything that will leave us with no more excuses and no more options. Perhaps we delay because we're afraid to fail. But God is trustworthy and patient with us. He will uphold us with His righteous right hand. The One who holds the answers to our questions will accompany us down the paths of His holy will, one step at a time.

Time to Think:

1. Have I ever resisted taking a step for God's kingdom because it didn't seem logical to me?

2. When I observe people making radical decisions (for instance, giving up a high-salary job) because they believe God wants them to, I tend to think that:

   _____ they're being foolish; God doesn't tell people to do things that don't make sense.

   _____ they're trying to compensate for sin in their past.

   _____ they're brave; no guts, no glory.

   _____ they're Spirit-filled to be able to sense God so strongly.

3. Where on the scale does my thinking fall as I make decisions?

What's best for me   What's best for God's kingdom

What Was Gideon Thinking?

Judges 6:11–40

He led the Israelite people to victory over the Amalekites and Midianites in an impressive display, but what Gideon is most known for are his creative methods of discerning God's will; when we think "Gideon," we think "fleece."

Was he a weakling or a wise man? Indecisive or just cautious? Perhaps we should give Gideon the benefit of the doubt. After all, God Himself was patient with Gideon as he prepared an offering as a test; the Angel of the Lord said, *"I will wait until you come back'"* (v. 18). God was willing to deal with Gideon's humanity, confirming three times that He was indeed calling Gideon to lead in a battle to defeat the Israelites' enemies. Gideon may have been hesitant to get to the starting line, but once he was certain of God's will, he fulfilled God's plan and made it into the Hebrews hall of faith (Hebrews 11:32).

God was gracious to Gideon, and He will be gracious to you. Ask God to confirm His will for your life, then run swiftly toward the path God shows you.

DAY 17: DISCERNING YOUR MOTIVES

Thought: Our mind decides the motive behind every action we take or word we say.

Challenge: Examine your motives behind every good deed and decide to do all for the glory of God.

As I write this, I am working to complete the tenth book that I've written or co-written. Each book has been a journey, and I've learned much about God, the Scripture, the writing process, and myself along the way. A few days ago, a colleague in India asked if I would mentor some of his writers for his Christian publishing company, and I thought, *What an opportunity! What would I want to share with a budding author?* As I mulled over the question in my mind and prayed, the answer came quickly and surprised me: Write only because you have a message to share. Don't write to sell books. Don't write to make money. Don't write to become famous. Don't write to impress people. Don't write to prove something to yourself or to others. Write only because God has put a word in your mind and it's burning the tips of your fingers to be typed out and shared with the world. Write for the right reasons. Write with the proper motives.

I have suffered—yes, suffered—through the agony of trying to do the right thing but with the wrong motives. Oh, what hard lessons these have been to learn. During these lessons, God has taken me through a refining process to mature me, helping me realize that He knows my thoughts and requires that I do everything for His glory, never for my own, and never out of fear, guilt, or selfishness.

One "motives lesson" that I recall occurred early in my speaking ministry when I toyed with taking my messages in a different direction. From the beginning, God had always laid on my heart a message to challenge women to surrender completely to the lordship of Christ. I'm a Matthew 16:24 kind of girl. But suddenly I began meeting women's ministry leaders who inquired about having me speak, and they would say, "Our ladies love to laugh; are you funny?" I felt the temptation to make just a little "shift" in my messages. I agonized with that decision, but I brought the suffering upon myself; I knew God designed me to deliver challenging messages, but I wanted to be liked. I wanted to be the one with the calling to make people laugh! I prayed over this decision, and in my gut I knew God was telling me to stay the course with my calling, but I kept convincing myself that the red light was yellow.

God knew my thoughts, and finally He hit me between the eyes with a direct message to check my motives: *"I charge you therefore before God and the Lord Jesus Christ, who will judge the living and the dead at His appearing and His kingdom: Preach the word! Be ready in season and out of season. Convince, rebuke, exhort, with all longsuffering and teaching. For the time will come when they will not endure sound doctrine, but according to their own desires, because they have itching ears, they will heap up for themselves teachers; and they will turn their ears away from the truth, and be turned aside to fables. But you be watchful in all things, endure afflictions, do the work of an evangelist, fulfill your ministry"* (2 Timothy 4:1–5). God's Word was crystal clear. My motive as a speaker could never be about pleasing people and fulfilling their expectations; I had to speak God's message to please Him alone and to fulfill His expectations.

What is done for the wrong motivation is drudgery. For instance, when we read our Bible daily only to be able to say that we've met our obligation, the study time feels like a chore. It's an albatross around our necks, like bondage. What is done to bring glory to God brings great joy, because we are exercising our freedom in Christ and we choose to honor Him with love, not obligation.

How can you be sure of your motives? These are thoughts that are deeply embedded, the kind of thoughts that we often ignore. In order to know the truth, we need God's Word to dig it out: *"For the word of God is living and powerful, and sharper than any two-edged sword, piercing even to the division of soul and spirit, and of joints and marrow, and is a discerner of the thoughts and intents of the heart"* (Hebrews 4:12). Second Timothy 4:1–5 was like a finger pointed directly at me about my speaking ministry, and I could not escape the truth that I so desperately needed to hear. Time and again in my life, I have experienced that same "finger" pointing at me during my morning Bible study time, as God has shown me from His Word when my intentions are askew from God's narrow path of holy living. God's Word is like a mirror that reflects back to me who I am, what I'm thinking, and what my motivation or intentions are. The Scripture's power to discern helps me peer beneath the surface, beyond where human eyes can see, to the truth of my thinking, and I am better for it.

As you face your next big decision, take careful consideration of your motives. When you can peel back the layers of your choice and see what is motivating you to cling to an option, you may find the decision becomes much easier as you release any option that is motivated by wrong thinking.

107

Time to Think:

1. A decision I am currently facing is _____ .
   As I think about this decision:

   Will this glorify God, or me?

   Am I motivated to get relief from a situation?

   Am I seeking the easiest way, or the best way?

   Am I operating in faith in a person, or faith in God?

2. How often am I receiving the benefits of Hebrews 4:12?

3. As I read James 1:21–24, I realize I need to:

4. I need to talk to God about my motivation for doing:

108

What Were Ananias and Sapphira Thinking?

Acts 4:37–5:11

Maybe it went something like this:

"That Barnabas sure did create a stir. I don't think a single person left our gathering today without first hugging his neck for his generous gift. I guess that's all we're going to hear about for awhile, how generous Barnabas is."

"Yeah, honey, but you've got to think: a lot of our other brothers and sisters in Christ have been giving large gifts, too. I'm starting to feel a little embarrassed that we've got that nice piece of property we've been holding onto for years, and I'm pretty sure that at least some of the apostles know about it. Do you think anyone is talking about us? Do you think we seem like tightwads?"

"Sapphira, you worry too much. Who cares what they think? It's ours, we can do what we want to with our possessions. No one is being pressured to sell land or treasures for the cause."

"Yes, but there certainly has been a trend of generosity, and Barnabas is like a hero! You, on the other hand, are a zero, and that makes me a zero too. Ananias, I don't want to give away everything we have, but we've got to do something."

"Well, a thought does come to mind. What if we sold the land and gave most of the profit, but we held back some for ourselves?"

"No way, Ananias! We're better off giving nothing and looking like we're poor than giving only a portion of the proceeds and looking stingy! 'Here, Peter. Here's a little something for the cause. We're stuffing our coffers with the rest!'"

"My dear wife, you're not thinking clearly. Who will know the total proceeds? If you and I agree . . . "

109

Ananias and Sapphira didn't suffer God's wrath because of the total amount given. The apostles weren't requiring that the early believers sell all of their possessions and give it to the church family. No, Ananias and Sapphira's sin was their act of deception. They tried to lie to God and test the Holy Spirit. What's more, they plotted to deceive the brethren because they wanted people to give them credit for giving their all. Their gift was nothing more than an attempt to elevate themselves, but their evil motivations became known to all when the two dropped dead at Peter's feet.

Do people have similar motives in the body of Christ today? Do Christians ever give less than a full tithe but boast about their tithing records? Do Christians ever sing hymns during worship services, but not pay attention to the lyrics closely enough to realize they're singing empty pledges to God? Do Christians ever attend worship services only out of obligation, and not to worship? Do Christians ever pontificate during small-group Bible study about living a life of faith, while knowing they don't think very often about God during the week? Do Christians ever do missions work or church work with one ear cocked to hear words of praise from their peers?

DAY 18: SORTING THROUGH A MAZE OF DECISIONS

Thought: Making a decision can seem like an endless flow of "what ifs," "if thens," and dead ends. However, God knows exactly what He wants you to do.

Challenge: Break down a decision into God-honoring considerations and ask Him to guide your thinking.

Do you remember studying flow charts in high school? The flow begins with one question, which then branches into two streams of possibilities based on your yes or no to the question, then question builds upon question, and soon you have a page covered with boxes, questions, and arrows. When I'm facing a life-altering decision, I find myself creating multiple mental flow charts. I get dizzy trying to control every possible outcome. I feel frustrated when I start leaning toward a decision, only to have it dead end at a point when I can't figure out how to make every detail work the way I want it to.

See if you relate to this:

I have to give up one of my hobbies. I could give up the book club. But if I'm no longer there to be in charge of the book club, the other ladies have said that they don't feel able to step up to lead. It's a vital ministry that appears to be hinging upon my decision. Plus, I was about to invite Jan to start coming to the book club, and she really needs to make new friends, so no, I won't give up the book club. I could give up aerobics. But I need the exercise to stay healthy, and it's a good chance to meet other women and minister to them. The issue is that I'm getting too busy on week nights, and aerobics is two nights a week. Well, maybe I should reconsider giving up the book club since that would free up one night a week for me, then I could continue with aerobics. Oh, but I can't do that because of Jan. But I could invite Jan to aerobics! Problem solved, I'll give up the book club. But I love all of those ladies, I started that group from scratch, I know they appreciate my leadership, I am certain that God knitted our hearts together. . . . OK, let's just start again. What else could I give up? And why again was I trying to give up one of my hobbies? Maybe I need to do nothing. This is getting too hard! Round and round I go, like a mouse lost in a maze, bumping into dead ends.

Making a serious decision can be exhausting, but God's Word gives us insight into how to approach the decision with baby steps, walking closer and closer to the center of God's will. Think about a decision that you currently face. No matter the choices before you, ask God to help you:

- Approach the decision as spiritual in nature. Decision making reveals who our master is, whether it's the Lord Jesus or the operations of this world. When the Israelite people had turned their backs on God and began worshipping the false god Baal, the prophet Elijah put them to the test and said to the people, *"How long will you falter between two opinions? If the Lord is God, follow Him, but if Baal, follow him"* (1 Kings 18:21). Step one in making a decision must be to decide to follow God's leadership above all, no matter what other factors are involved. If He is our God, we follow Him. Period.

  Wouldn't making choices be more convenient if we could lump everything into two categories: spiritual and nonspiritual? *Yes, God cares about how much I give to feed the poor, but no, God doesn't care what kind of car I buy . . .* unless what kind of car I buy affects how much I can give to the poor. Our sin nature is strong and the flesh is weak, so we must boldly come before God for every decision, realizing that we're capable of talking ourselves into believing we can do whatever pleases us and God "won't mind." Jesus said, *"No servant can serve two masters; for either he will hate the one and love the other, or else he will be loyal to the one and despise the other. You cannot serve God and mammon"* (Luke 16:13). Truly He is Lord of our lives when He is Lord of our decisions.

- Come to the Lord with humility, and be patient for His response. When we pray, we're invited to enter the throne room of God to bring our questions before the King. Imagine yourself in that throne room. Look around you. You have entered into God's holy presence, the Eternal One who sits on a heavenly throne, and you have asked Him for guidance. Now what will you do? Will you rush the King? No, with humility you will bend the knee in His presence and silently, patiently wait for Him to speak.

We ask God for leadership, and then we must wait. Humility is a great companion of patience; we acknowledge that God has authority, thus we will jump when God calls, and never the reverse. In God's timing, we will have an assurance of His will. Until then, we don't have to continue running through the mouse maze, we don't have to keep trying to figure out every detail, we don't need to pace before His throne . . . we wait with quiet confidence. Scheming only complicates our thinking and leads us away from loving God: *"A man's heart plans his way, but the LORD directs his steps"* (Proverbs 16:9).

- Listen. We ask God to guide our decisions, and then we stop talking. We stand still, and we listen. God has made a promise: *"And though the Lord gives you the bread of adversity and the water of affliction, yet your teachers will not be moved into a corner anymore, but your eyes shall see your teachers. Your ears shall hear a word behind you, saying, 'This is the way, walk in it,' whenever you turn to the right hand or whenever you turn to the left"* (Isaiah 30:20–21). We listen for the whispers of God to fall gently upon our ears.

In my years of offering counsel to people dealing with a wide range of decisions, I have found that one question trumps the rest: "Am I called to do this?" When we can answer that question without any consideration of further "what ifs," "what thens," or "yeah buts," peace will wash over us and we

113

will know what God has said. There's no more need to run through mazes. When we know the answer to that question, nothing else matters, because we know that God will work out all the resulting details. Instead of thinking, *If I do this, what about this repercussion, and that repercussion?* we can declare boldly, "God has called me to this decision. I am going to go in that direction no matter what." Now you're thinking clearly. Now you're loving God.

Time to Think:

1. When faced with a difficult decision, I:
   _____ write a pros and cons list.
   _____ decide not to decide.
   _____ ask my peers what they suggest I do.
   _____ run through a maze of options.
   _____ Other: _____

2. What percent of the time do I seek God's face for decisions?
   _____ percent

3. What percent of the time do I wait patiently for God to give me an answer? _____ percent

4. How often in my life have I heard God's voice saying to me, "This is the way, walk in it"?

5. What is the decision facing me today? What do I need to ask God about this decision?

What Was Ezra Thinking?

Ezra 8:21–23

God hadn't made it an easy journey, but He had carved a path of twists and turns and provided for the Israelites to be successful. Their quest was to rebuild the temple, and Ezra found himself and the people now at a juncture of decision. Ezra called the people to humble themselves before the Lord. They needed holy guidance more than they needed food.

Ezra realized the gravity of the decision before them. He camped out and wouldn't move until He heard from God. For the men of leadership, their lives would be forever changed by each step they took toward their future. But this decision would also impact their little ones, the next generation; Ezra longed to leave a God-honoring blueprint for them to follow. And as for their possessions, Ezra would not be flippant about their resources. God had given them everything, and each coin and piece of wood needed to be used precisely as God desired.

Do you long for God's direction more than anything else? Are you feeling the weight of the burden? For you, your family, and your legacy, come humbly before your God.

116

DAY 19: ON SECOND THOUGHT

Thought: Part of making God-honoring decisions is sticking with those decisions.

Challenge: Let go of negative thoughts that are luring you back to square one.

I had both hands on the steering wheel for the last time. I was en route to purchase a cute little red sports car that was exactly what I wanted. I was young with no children, and I figured this was my last shot at a sports car for a very long time. The car was on hold, the price had been settled, the paperwork had started, and I was 20 minutes away from my dream car. I was ready to seize the moment! Or was I? I looked over at the mahogany-esque dashboard of my vehicle I was about to trade in—ah, the memories. This was the first car I had ever owned. My husband bought it for me, and he had worked it out to buy me just the one I wanted—metallic gray, low mileage, CD player (yes, it was a big deal back then), and that beautiful mahogany-looking dashboard that made me feel like a million bucks. I didn't care that it was high gloss plastic when we bought the car, and somehow as I was on my way to trade it in, I loved the fake mahogany as much as the day we bought it.

117

I felt sick. Suddenly I wasn't so sure about my decision, and the car purchase haunted me for days. I finally confessed my feelings to my husband and he said two words I had never heard before, this description of a state of mind: buyer's remorse.

No doubt, it's a challenge to make a wise decision. You pray, seek wise council, weigh the options, search the Scriptures, think through the situation thoroughly, and then that moment comes when you make a decision. You seal the deal and make it real when you say it aloud to someone else, and now you're locked into your choice. It feels good to make a decision! But is the battle over? Not necessarily, not if you're willing to keep the wheels turning and obsess about your choices a little while longer. When you've made a decision, you must be stalwart to avoid the pitfalls.

- Second-guessing is just guessing. If you've prayed about a decision and felt God's leadership, you have no reason to doubt your choice. Let go of it with your mind. God is not the author of confusion (1 Corinthians 14:33), and He won't lead you astray. Refuse to play the "what if" game and rest in your decision. A God-honoring decision is based on faith when you initially make the choice, and it's faith that helps you stay the course without wavering.

- The grass is always greener in your former lawn. In the early years when my three children were newborn, one year old, and three years old, I had to force my eyeballs not to roll when people would tell me, "Enjoy them while they're young, honey, because it will all be over in a flash. I wish mine were still little and crawling around in diapers. Those were the best years of my life." Really? Emptying diaper pails, dealing with tantrums, warming bottles, midnight feedings, having to plan strategically when to take a quick shower, never having time to read, being exhausted by 10:00 A.M., spoon-feeding babies at the table while your plate of food gets cold . . . that was the best? Well, that's probably not what they meant. They were remembering footy pajamas, baby powder, sweet cuddle times, and all that is precious about having a baby. It truly was wonderful. But it wasn't easy.

  Add a dash of imagination, a spoonful of romanticism, a pinch of convenient forgetfulness, stir with the arms of your rose-colored glasses, and what you've created is a half-truth, half-fantasy about the way things used to be. When you make a decision, the initial feelings can be euphoric as you experience the newness of it all. It's the "new car smell" effect or the "honeymoon phase" of a new job, a new relationship, or a new lifestyle. But no matter how right the decision was for you, the honeymoon period will eventually end. Even though God led you to move to a different department at work, you eventually will come to realize that your new supervisor has a temper problem. Or the decision to stay home from work to care for your little ones seemed like a dream come true and God's gift to you, but eventually you'll have days of feeling underappreciated. On those days of challenge, fight the urge to indulge thoughts about the good old days. God gave you wisdom to make a choice, but He never promised that walking into that decision would make life problem free. He has only promised to be with you. And going back, as good as it may seem to you as you peer into the past, would only be a disaster.

- Don't revisit your sin. Life is lived moving forward. In the past might be poor decisions, temptation, immaturity, sin— but today is a new day. You've made your decision to move forward with God, and the old ways are not for you anymore. When you choose to live as Christ, there's no looking back.

    The only famous pillar of salt in history used to be a living, breathing woman who insisted on looking back: Lot's wife. When God poured out His wrath upon Sodom and Gomorrah, He was gracious to spare Lot and his wife. As the couple was fleeing their former home, a wicked, morally depraved city, their minds should have been filled with wonder that God had spared them. Their thoughts should have been of gratitude toward God and appreciation that they still had a future ahead of them. Their old lives were going up in flames and there was nothing left for them in that city. Why look back? Maybe it was memories. Maybe it was nostalgia. Maybe it was a fondness for the pleasures of the flesh that the sinful city had offered her in the past. Lot's wife felt a strong tug

119

that she did not resist, and she gazed upon her past *just one more time*. The effects of sin was the last thing she saw as she glanced back to see the smoldering city.

There's no looking back to your life before Christ, but there's also no looking back to yesterday's weaknesses. Did God convict you to give up drinking? Don't talk yourself into believing it's OK to start drinking again. Has God called you to end an immoral relationship? Don't entertain thoughts of going back. You will experience sustained spiritual growth when God leads you to a higher moral plain and you make the choice to never back down.

Your mind has many vital functions to do today. You don't have time to continue revisiting decisions that you've already settled with God. Free up your grey matter to love God with confidence in His leadership of your life.

Time to Think:

1. How often do I second-guess myself about decisions?

   _____ Always

   _____ Sometimes

   _____ Rarely

2. When I second-guess myself, it's usually because:

   _____ Someone has criticized my choice. (Why does that bother me?)

   _____ I don't believe in myself; I expect to make a mess of things. (Why do I think so little of myself?)

   _____ I'm afraid of losing everything. (What is the source of my fears?)

   _____ I have a hard time hearing God's voice. (How can I position myself to better discern God's voice?)

3. Proverbs 26:11 challenges me to keep my resolve to:

4. The next time my resolve weakens about a decision I've made as a follower of Christ, I am going to:

121

What Was Jochebed Thinking?

Exodus 2:1–10

Jochebed faced a decision that no woman should ever have to face. The Egyptians were killing baby boys, and she had hidden her newborn son for as long as she could without being detected. Something had to be done. Not to decide would be to decide his death, because the child was too active to be hidden any more. Jochebed showed amazing courage when she placed her child in a basket among the reeds. Imagine that moment when her hands let go of the child. Next came the decision to take her fingers off the basket. Then to stand up . . . next to step back . . . and then to walk away.

God rewarded the courage of Jochebed to make a gut-wrenching decision and then follow through with her resolve. God loved Jochebed, and He loved that little baby in that basket. God loves you too. It's time for you to move forward with your decisions. Take your hands off the past, step back, and walk away. As you walk away from the past, you are walking toward your future.

DAY 20: NAVIGATING CHANGE

Thought: You cannot control all of the changes that occur in your life, but you can determine how you'll respond to those changes.

Challenge: When change comes, decide how to respond based on your belief in the goodness and the sovereignty of God.

I've been to some rather exotic places in the world, and I've eaten my share of mystery meat, bland soup, and what was frankly akin to bean paste, but I have never longed for American food more than when traveling in the Czech Republic. The Czech food and my taste buds never seemed to get along. After several days of eating for nourishment purposes only, I was beside myself when my eyes fell upon golden arches. McDonald's! It was a sight for sore eyes and very unhappy taste buds. I stepped to the counter and could not wait to wrap my fingers around a burger smothered in ketchup. My mouth was getting really pumped with anticipation. Finally my tray arrived, and when I took that initial bite of burger, my mind could not believe what my mouth was telling it. Somehow, some way, they had managed to change the taste of my beloved burger. It was cruel irony.

123

It's no small feat what the restaurant industry has managed to pull off marvelously, at least within the United States. You can enter any drive-through in America and order a cheeseburger from your favorite fast-food establishment, and before you ever pull back the wrapper and indulge, you already know exactly what the burger is going to taste like. Thousands of people will eat that same menu item from hundreds of restaurants spread out geographically from coast to coast, and they will each have the same dining experience. They can return the next day, the next week, or six months later, and the food will taste exactly the same. Amazing. And that's the way we like it!

But life is not a drive-through menu. Things change. People fall in love. People fall out of love. Jobs phase out. Technology becomes outdated. Babies are born. People die. Gadgets break. Health circumstances deteriorate. Weight shifts. Life is in a state of flux. Life has no pause button, and time rolls along to usher more changes whether we're ready to adjust or not.

Life decisions are often prompted by change. Thinking about making a change can be exciting if we're considering a new opportunity that we can accept or decline, but most change falls into a different category: that which is forced upon us. When we're required by life circumstances to make a change, we often struggle because it tears down the paper-thin walls of our fantasy world where we enjoy a false sense of security. Just when we think that everything's under control and we can set our minds on cruise control to indulge in some frivolities, we get blindsided by a change in situation and we have to rethink our lives all over again.

When change is forced upon us, the only choice we have in the matter is how we will respond. Our minds have the option of which route to take as we navigate change:

- Depression and fear. Depression and fear happen when we doubt the goodness of God and the sovereignty of God. In Isaiah 43:18–19, God says, *"Do not remember the former things, nor consider the things of old. Behold, I will do a new thing, now it shall spring forth; shall you not know it? I will even make a road in the wilderness and rivers in the desert."* A new thing—that means change! When God brings forth something new, it can happen very much like a plant springing forth out of the ground: It can seem like the change came out of nowhere and it takes us by surprise, but God knew exactly where, when, and how it would unfold. God says, *"Shall you not know it?"* Look up! Look forward! Expect God to have a purpose for the changes He brings to your life. Believe that God is faithful.

- Anger and complaining. When we choose anger and complaining, we forfeit focus and favor. We stop thinking rationally and we're tossed about by waves of strong, destructive emotions. It's human nature to first think about how a change affects us personally. We turn the situation over and over in our minds, trying to figure out what God is doing to us. But sometimes in order to get past the frustration and anger, we have to consider the situation from a different perspective. Perhaps not every change is solely about us. Perhaps God is creating a change in our lives in order to bring about growth in someone else's.

• Acceptance and hope. God is always purposing to make you a better you. Let Him refine you. Let Him redefine you. Let Him reshape you.

Solomon was the wisest man who ever lived, and he learned to accept change. Think deeply about the words of the king:

125

> To everything there is a season,
> A time for every purpose under heaven:
> A time to be born,
> And a time to die;
> A time to plant,
> And a time to pluck what is planted;
> A time to kill,
> And a time to heal;
> A time to break down,
> And a time to build up;
> A time to weep,
> And a time to laugh;
> A time to mourn,
> And a time to dance;
> A time to cast away stones,

And a time to gather stones;
A time to embrace,
And a time to refrain from embracing;
A time to gain,
And a time to lose;
A time to keep,
And a time to throw away;
A time to tear,
And a time to sew;
A time to keep silence,
And a time to speak;
A time to love,
And a time to hate;
A time of war,
And a time of peace.
—ECCLESIASTES 3:1–8

Time to Think:

1. The hardest change I've ever faced was when:

When it happened, my thoughts were that:

2. The biggest change I'm facing right now is:

My thoughts about it are best described as:
_____ Depression and fear
_____ Anger and complaining
_____ Acceptance and fear
_____ Other: _____

3. Do I indulge a false sense of security? Do I have a false sense of control?

4. How will I love God with my mind the next time I am surprised with a life change?

What Was Mary Thinking?

Luke 1:26–38

Forget the daydreams of a quiet life in Nazareth. Good-bye to plans for the perfect wedding. God had spoken, and His plans were nothing like Mary could have imagined. The bridal bliss she had been hoping for since she was a little girl was not going to come together for Mary; or at least, not in the traditional fashion. Unwed Mary was going to have a baby. Her plans, her relationships, her life—everything was about to change.

Mary said, *"Let it be to me"* (v. 38). What an astonishing relinquishment of control. She was choosing to be putty in the Potter's hands. Mary was fully releasing the reins of her life to God, but not only that, she was telling God that she wanted her life to turn out *exactly* as God had planned. Her Maker had thrown up a U-turn sign, and Mary was content to let God navigate her life in a new direction.

Accepting change is coming to the place when you can say in truth, "Let it be to me." Be still before the Lord and embrace His leadership. Wherever He leads, you can know that He is taking you in the right direction.

chapter five
Thoughts of You

For as he thinks in his heart, so is he.
—PROVERBS 23:7—

You have some definite thoughts about yourself. It's time to think again. Your mind belongs to God, and every thought you have should pass through the filter of truth that is defined by all that God has said. God has had much to say about you. Perhaps you thought you knew all there is to know about yourself, but on second thought . . . what is the truth about you? Proverbs 23:7 is both a promise and a warning; what you think about yourself will largely define who you will choose to be. Are you thinking what God's thinking?

DAY 21: WHAT MAKES YOU SO SPECIAL

Thought: Society measures the worth of a person with a different set of values than God.

Challenge: Measure your worth by God's standards.

What do you think about yourself? Are you good-looking, average, or unattractive? You've got your mind made up, and how you evaluate yourself is based on what society has trained you to think. In America, we try to have trim bodies because we've been programmed to believe that trim is beautiful, but did you know that in West Africa a large rear end makes for a beautiful woman? Interesting. Today, we bake our skin in the sun or the tanning bed because we've bought into the idea that tanned skin is attractive, but the beautiful princesses of medieval times kept their skin as pale as possible; in their society, pale was in and tan was out.

What would you say about your intellect? Your charisma? Your talent? All your life you've been receiving messages from parents, teachers, peers, and supervisors who have let you know what they think of you. They have evaluated you by society's measuring stick, and chances are you've met at least a few people who let you know you didn't measure up. The old "sticks and stones" poem is not true; words do hurt, and if you're not careful you'll absorb those words and let them shape what you believe about yourself.

In my youth, I struggled with my identity. My family moved often because of my dad's work, and every school meant a reshaping of my identity. I felt the scrutiny of my peers, and within a few weeks I could expect a label. Through the years, those labels had me all over the map. In seventh grade, I was on top of the world because I believed I was one of the nicest, smartest, most popular girls in school. Then my family moved to New England for my eighth-grade year, and my social status shifted to the opposite pole. Suddenly I was the backwards, unsophisticated girl with the dumb Southern accent who couldn't find a friend. Even the guidance counselor said I was intellectually inferior, and told my mother and me that I could

130

expect to go from making A's in the South to barely passing in the North. It was a year in my youth that rocked my world. I wasn't sure who I was anymore.

When you base your worth on what others say about you, you're always one remark away from losing your confidence. Your friends want you to be the best you possible, but based on their perspective of what defines "best." Your boss wants you to shine based on his or her expectations for a good employee. Your in-laws have a definite standard that they want you to live up to, which is what they believe it takes for you and their child to live happily ever after. Even your pet would tell you, if he could talk, about what he believes would make you the best master ever. You cannot live up to all of these separate sets of standards, and many of these standards are flawed, unreasonable, or based on selfish motives.

131

Only God can offer you a fair and accurate assessment of you. While your peers, no matter how well-meaning, cannot help but have an ulterior motive for their assessment, God gains nothing nor loses anything based on you; He stands secure in His identity as the sovereign Ruler of the universe. He doesn't need you to fit into His mold to make Him feel good about Himself, and He doesn't need you to be a winner in order to make Him look good. He's God. He also isn't swayed by popular opinion, fads, or cultural shifts. He does not change, so His standards never change. You can also count on God to look beyond your outward appearance. God Himself has said, *"For the LORD does not see as man sees; for man looks at the outward appearance, but the LORD looks at the heart"* (1 Samuel 16:7). He won't be charmed by your good looks and youthful glow, nor will He think less of your abilities when wrinkles begin to define your face. And at the same token, God knows that not everyone with gray hair is wise, nor is every young person foolish. God

Chapter 5 • Thoughts of You

looks directly into the essence of who you are, and He knows the real you.

No one knows you better than God, and no one values you more than He does. God made you in His very own image (Genesis 1:26). God made you and formed you (Isaiah 44:2). You are His special creation, and that makes you of great worth. But not only did God care enough to make you, He takes a particular interest in you. You aren't just another face in a sea of faces. You aren't person no. 577,624,518,967,334 to God. No, God has always known you. Before you were born, God knew you and had already set you apart (Jeremiah 1:5). Make no mistake, you are a special person, and for this reason: You are special to God.

Tucked away in your mind are file cabinets filled with every compliment, report card, knowing look, high five, taunting jeer, and rejection letter you've ever received. Purge the files. Take a new memo. God has said, *"I have loved you with an everlasting love"* (Jeremiah 31:3).

Time to Think:

1. The comments I still remember that have hurt me the most through the years were:

2. I struggle with my self-worth most in the area of:
   _____ Physical appearance
   _____ Talent
   _____ Intelligence
   _____ Social status
   _____ Education
   _____ Creativity
   _____ Others' expectations in my family role
   _____ Other: _____

3. To think that God knows who I am and knew me before I was ever born makes me realize that:

4. I can't fully love God with my mind when I think very little of myself because:

5. The one damaging thought I have about myself that I want to let go of is:

133

What Was Mephibosheth Thinking?

2 Samuel 9

Dead dog. Not exactly flattering words for a man to use about himself. Mephibosheth was of royal blood, the grandson of King Saul, but that regime was short-lived. Saul was dead, Mephibosheth's father Jonathan was also dead, and the new king was searching for any remaining bloodline from Saul's family. It was reasonable for Mephibosheth to assume he was as good as dead, given that most kings executed the remaining family of the former king.

King David wasn't like most kings. God had given David the throne, and when God grants a man a position, he can feel secure in his role. No, David wasn't running scared, trying to kill off any potential competition for the throne; David wanted to bless Mephibosheth. David wanted to treat him like royalty. David wanted Mephibosheth to be grafted into the family.

Like Mephibosheth, we aren't obvious candidates to be granted seats at God's royal table. Mephibosheth was lame in both feet, a tragic circumstance for a man living in a culture who had no use for the physically disabled, and we also have our own disabilities. We come before God with weaknesses, and we are unable to wow Him with our skills or talents. We come before God, and when we see Him in His glory, we utter, *"What is your servant, that you should look upon such a dead dog as I?"* (v. 8).

The story of David and Mephibosheth is a beautiful image of God's grace, because God draws us out in order to bless us. Only because He wants to, God invites us to sit at His table. He grafts us into His family because it brings Him pleasure. He chooses to value us, and this grand elevation to the status of children of God makes us people of honor and worth. He has declared it. Let us come to the table.

DAY 22: BELIEVING WHAT GOD HAS SAID ABOUT YOU

Thought: God has spoken great words of affirmation about everyone who believes in Jesus Christ as Lord.

Challenge: Believe what God has said about who you are in Christ.

Today's chapter is going to either inspire you or hurt your feelings. No matter who you are, everything you read in day 21 is true. God loves you, He formed you, He values you, He knows you—this much is true of every person ever born. But today we must make a distinction. Day 21 dealt with what God has said about everyone who has been born, but today we must deal with what God has said about everyone who has been born *again.*

Not everyone has been born again. Jesus had a conversation in John 3:3–21 with a man named Nicodemus. Jesus told Nicodemus, *"'Unless one is born again, he cannot see the kingdom of God'"* (v. 3). Jesus is making a distinction between those who have become followers of Christ and those who have not. The Bible is filled with beautiful words that describe the one who is a follower of Christ.

- Child of God (John 1:12). We become children of God when we are adopted into God's family through placing our faith in Jesus Christ (Ephesians 1:5). As a child of God, we receive rights and privileges as sons and daughters. We become heirs of God (Galatians 4:7).

- More than a conqueror (Romans 8:37). God has plans of victory for us. We are not the defeated, but the victorious. We are God's champions.
- The salt of the earth (Matthew 5:13). God can use us in many practical ways to bring help and healing to others.
- The light of the world (Matthew 5:14). In a world filled with darkness, we bring light so that others can see to escape. Light reveals the truth.
- A city set upon a hill (Matthew 5:14). Like the relief of a weary traveler who has been wandering through the desert and is now overjoyed to see a city on a hill in the distance, so we also can bring relief to those who are spiritually weary and in need. We offer the lost and hurting hospitality and shelter, and we introduce them to the Lord Jesus.
- A precious jewel belonging to God (Malachi 3:17). Some days we may look more like a diamond in the rough, but God declares that we are rare and exquisite gems, His treasure.
- Forgiven (Colossians 2:13). Our guilt is removed from us.
- A member of the royal priesthood (1 Peter 2:9). We can boldly come before God's throne and speak to Him with the authority of a member of His holy and royal priesthood (Hebrews 4:16). We have been given the right to serve God with nearness to Him; we are in His inner circle.
- Chosen to be one of God's holy and special people (1 Peter 2:9). We are set apart and peculiar in nature. We are different from the world. We stand apart, and that's a good thing, because we are distinctly different from the children of wrath (Ephesians 2:3).

136

- Gifted to minister (1 Peter 4:10). We've been given a gift, a spiritual gift that cannot be bought or sold, and that gift can only be given by God Himself and only received by His people. Our gifts enable us to serve as ministers in Jesus' name.
- Thoroughly equipped (2 Timothy 3:17). Through the equipping that comes from God's Word, we can do the good works of God. We lack absolutely nothing.

This listing is a mere fraction of the affirming words God has used to describe His people.

The Bible also describes the one who is not a Christ follower: *"He who does not believe is condemned already, because he has not believed in the name of the only begotten Son of God"* (John 3:18). If you aren't a born-again Christian, don't be offended; every person stands guilty as the enemy of God before coming to Christ (Romans 5:10). The good news is that we don't have to remain in that state of estrangement. Don't be confused; even if you haven't come to Christ as your Savior, God does indeed know you and love you, and desires that you become His precious jewel. God proved it by sending His Son to die for you. And don't be fooled; remember Nicodemus, the religious man whom Jesus told that he must be born again? Nicodemus was a Pharisee, a ruler of the Jews, a deeply religious man who was active in temple worship and a follower of the law. Today's words of affirmation and strength aren't reserved for the religious, but they are reserved for the righteous who live by faith in Jesus Christ.

Do today's words of affirmation apply to you? If so, think carefully about how you define your identity. Be cautious not to define yourself by your vocation, otherwise you'll have an identity crisis if you lose your job or when you retire. Be sure

137

that you're not defining yourself by your role in your family relationships, or else you might find yourself in a heap on the floor if your spouse should suddenly be taken from you, or even when your children move out of the house. Don't be consumed by your ministry titles, because even these might be temporary and are subject to change. Who you are isn't what you do, what you look like, the role you play in your family, or your function in a business. Who you are isn't about your title on a name plate that sits on your desk, or how many zeros rest beside your name on a ledger at the bank. As a child of God, who you are is in Christ. When you accept your true identity, this truth changes the reality of how you think about everything.

Time to Think:

1. As you look at the many titles and descriptions God has given to you as a believer, do you find any of these titles difficult to accept? Why?

2. Which description means the most to you?

3. What is the difference between embracing your life roles to do your best, versus letting those roles define you?

What Was Moses Thinking?

Exodus 3

If any man ever had the potential for an identity crisis, it was Moses. He had been taken from his Hebrew home as a very young child and was raised by the Egyptian Pharaoh's daughter. His roots were among the Israelite slaves who called out to Jehovah God, but his formative years were spent as an adopted child of the Egyptian aristocracy who worshipped gods made with man's hands. Was Moses a noble or a slave? Was he a rich man or a poor man? Was he an oppressor or a member of the oppressed? His dual identities clashed one day when he saw an Egyptian taskmaster beating a Hebrew slave, and in a fit of rage Moses killed the Egyptian. His conflicted feelings must have only deepened when the Hebrew slaves only showed contempt for him after his murderous act, and then Pharaoh also rejected him and sought to take his life. Moses fled.

Moses made a new life for himself. He went to a new land, found a wife, and settled down to have a family. Now he was simply Moses: husband, father, and shepherd. He was content with these titles.

But God had other plans. God appeared to Moses and asked him to return to the place where he would once again have to face the conflict of his identity. Moses balked at first, asking, *"Who am I that I should go to Pharaoh?"* (v. 11), but God reassured Moses that he was just the man to serve as liaison between the Israelites and Pharaoh.

In time, Moses would see more clearly his identity, but his first step of faith was to believe that God knew him and had equipped him to fulfill his calling. Have you taken that step of faith? Do you believe what God has said about you?

DAY 23: TRUE HUMILITY

Thought: We are of great worth to God, and so is everyone else.

Challenge: Think of yourself with humility, of others with thoughtfulness, and of God with meekness.

It's a tricky thing to have accurate thoughts about ourselves. For the past two days, we've been reevaluating our perspective on our identity and worth in order to think of ourselves with all the value and worth that God has declared over us. But there's another direction we must consider about our thoughts of self. In his letter to the Romans, Paul wrote: *"For I say, through the grace given to me, to everyone who is among you, not to think of himself more highly than he ought to think"* (12:3). Whether it's self-depravation or self-exaltation, both directions of thinking are "self-ish" in nature and a deviation from how God has taught us to think about ourselves.

My mom used to call it being too big for your britches. When her children started thinking they were too sophisticated to wear hand-me-downs, too old to follow instructions, or too important to help around the house, Mom stepped in with a dose of reality. We were loved, cherished, respected, and valued in our home, but none of us was more important than the rest of the family.

When we indulge in thinking too highly of ourselves, automatically everyone else falls beneath us in priority. We feel entitled, and we grab what we want. We feel important, and we expect others to meet our needs. We are sure we're right, and we never consider that others may have something valuable to contribute. We are thinking of ourselves, and we're thinking

141

of ways to stay on top of the heap where we've positioned ourselves.

Haughty thinking has been the ruin of many a man. Jesus told the story of two sons who struggled with a high opinion of themselves (Luke 15:11–32). The younger son went to his father and demanded to receive his inheritance now. He didn't feel that he should have to wait until his father's death to be granted his father's money, and he went into a far country and spent all the money on himself in riotous living. When the foolish son had been humbled by hunger and complete destitution, he came to his senses and returned home to beg his father to let him be his servant. He realized he had acted so poorly at home that he had forfeited his right to be treated like a son anymore.

As he neared his father's house, the father surprised him by running the distance to greet him with a hug and kiss. The younger son began his confessional speech of humility, but the father restored him fully. The father threw a great celebration because he was grateful that his son was home once again. The younger son had fallen from his place of self-elevation, but he had learned a valuable lesson in humility.

The older son had his own set of pride issues. It appeared at first that he was the humble son, because he was different from his brother. The older son had stayed at home and continued to serve in his father's household. He hadn't been demanding or rebellious against his father. But when the younger son came home and the father celebrated, the older son's pride was uncovered. He asked his father, "Why do you throw a party for him and not me? I have been the faithful son to you all these years, but you've never killed a goat for me to make merry with my friends." As long as he felt secure in his relationship with his father, the older son was compliant and faithful. However, as soon as he felt that his younger brother was getting attention that only he deserved as the loyal son, he was overcome with anger and pride. The older son felt a strong sense of entitlement because he had "earned" the right to be his father's favorite. In the end we see that both sons had fallen into pride and self-exaltation. What heartbreak for this father of two sons who both thought too highly of themselves.

And imagine the heartbreak for Jesus when His very own disciples were arguing amongst themselves over which of them was greatest of all (Luke 22:24). Of all the things these men had to talk about, they wanted to discuss their greatness. All 12 of them had walked with the Son of God for three years. They had witnessed true perfection in Jesus Christ, and they should have realized that they each fell grossly short of the glory of God. It was their privilege to be near the Lord and to exalt His name to all mankind, but for the disciples, it wasn't enough. They knew they weren't as great as Jesus, but each of them believed he was better than his peers, and each of them was willing to call himself best.

As we read about the disciples' dispute, their behavior seems childish and shortsighted to us. How could they possibly argue over who was best among them when clearly Jesus had taught them to be humble through His powerful example as the Suffering Servant? However, before we point a finger too quickly at the disciples, we also must examine our own thinking and search for hints of prideful thoughts. We know we aren't perfect like Jesus, but deep down, do we think we're better than most people? Do we think we're right most of the time? Do we feel entitled? Are we proud of ourselves? It's hard to think about exalting the name of Jesus Christ when we're busy trying to make a name for ourselves. Think it over.

143

Time to Think:

1. What is the evidence in my life that I sometimes indulge in prideful thoughts?

   _____ I evaluate others' work in my mind and think about how I could do better.

   _____ I have been accused of being a know-it-all.

   _____ I feel slighted when I'm not selected for honors or positions of leadership.

   _____ I will cut in front of others in line when I'm in a hurry.

   _____ I frequently get fed up with others' incompetency.

   _____ I like to be noticed.

   _____ When I am unhappy with the way I'm being treated, I often say or think, "It's not fair."

2. Jesus said, *"Whoever exalts himself will be humbled, and he who humbles himself will be exalted"* (Matthew 23:12). God has humbled me by:

3. God is bringing to my mind that I must not think that I am too good to _____ .

144

What Were James and John Thinking?

Mark 10:35–45

It was a gutsy move. Twelve men were in Jesus' inner circle, and they all had the potential to be Christ's number two man when He took His rightful place on the throne. Had Jesus been investing a little more time in Peter lately? Was Matthew becoming Jesus' favorite? Was that Andrew they saw lingering after dinner last night to talk to Jesus privately? The 12 men had been arguing over who was greatest, and each of them wanted to be in Jesus' inner circle. James and John decided it was time to strike.

They wouldn't have made such a bold request of Jesus without talking it over with one another first. They were brothers and surely they must have felt destined for greatness. Would they lose out if Peter went to Jesus first, or Judas, or one of the others? No, they couldn't let that happen. They wanted a seat of glory with Jesus. They wanted the highest position available underneath the Christ, and the other ten men could find another seat. They asked to be exulted. They jockeyed for position, and Jesus humbled them.

Solomon was a king, and he knew much about people who sought power and position for themselves. Solomon wrote, *"To seek one's own glory is not glory"* (Proverbs 25:27). Glory is not to be seized. It is granted by God, who has plainly explained His methods: *"Humble yourselves in the sight of the Lord, and He will lift you up"* (James 4:10).

145

DAY 24: THE END OF SELF-CENTERED THINKING

Thought: Our thoughts of self often conflict with thoughts of how to help others.

Challenge: Think of the needs of others before your own.

"Despite what you think, the world does not revolve around you." Have you heard that expression? It's a response to that flesh nature that prompts us to position ourselves as the very center of the universe and look around us to think of every situation from the perspective of how it affects "me." And unfortunately, we all have a propensity to do it. We watch the news and learn of a skirmish in the Middle East, and our first thought is, *I guess gas prices are going up again.* Never mind the families being torn apart and the grief of every mother who lost a son in the fighting. We hear that the company is laying off people in the warehouse, and we think, *I hope they don't start axing people in accounting, because I cannot afford to lose this job.* We give no thought to the poor chap whose wife is pregnant and he just lost his paycheck. God's people don't want to be self-centered, but our thoughts of self often consume us and keep us from ever having thoughts of the hurts, desires, and needs of others.

My son recently experienced a collision of what's best for others against what he wanted, and his conflict of interest caused him troubles in his prayer life. Our family had been praying for weeks for a missions team serving among an unreached people in West Africa, and John Mark had particularly prayed in earnest for the team's efforts to reach the lost. One day we received word from the field that the team needed us to pray for rain for Saturday. The community was planning a villagewide animal sacrifice on Saturday to appease the spirits, and the team was asking God to rain on those plans. I just knew that John Mark would be thrilled to make such a bold request of God, but instead he hesitated to begin his prayers. I was curious to know what was holding him in deep thought until finally he turned to me and said, "Mom, do you think we could ask God to only make it rain in Africa on Saturday? I was really hoping that I could go outside and play this weekend." At least he was honest. If God brought rain, John Mark felt it would cost him something. He knew he shouldn't think of himself first, but he would be really happy if God could help the missions team and preserve his own playdate at the same time. Bless his heart, I couldn't act shocked that John Mark was thinking about how rain in Africa might affect his day. How many times have I heard about a situation and then privately thought about how to maneuver the circumstances so that I would not be sucked in and be the loser? In those moments, I was willing to pray, help, or give to the cause, but couldn't I figure out a way to not be inconvenienced in the process?

Paul wrote, "*Let each of you look out not only for his own interests, but also for the interests of others*" (Philippians 2:4), and also, "*Let no one seek his own, but each one the other's well-being*" (1 Corinthians 10:24). In any given situation, we'll think more like Christ when we consider how others are affected by the problem instead of dwelling on what it's doing to us. And when we begin to realize that the people around us are also hurting and suffering through the situation, we'll be more apt to look out for their interests, putting ourselves last, and thus obey the law of Christ.

Jesus is our example. He left His throne on high and became poor for our sakes, that we might become rich with the treasures of heaven (2 Corinthians 8:9). He left heaven to walk the dusty earth because it was in our best interest that He come to the earth to die in our place. And as His earthly ministry was winding to its end, Jesus knew that the Cross was ahead of Him; He didn't look forward to the suffering and shame, and He prayed in agony with great sweat drops of blood as He talked with His Father just moments before His arrest (Luke 22:44). Yet He yielded to the Father's will that He suffer and die on a cruel cross because He loved us and was willing to lay down His life so that we might live. Jesus is the antithesis of self-centered thinking. His example compels us to step out of the center and to seek the welfare of others, that we might glorify Christ in our thoughts toward others.

Time to Think:

1. Which better describes my thought life?

   _____ I think about how to get blessings.

   _____ I think about how to bless others.

2. Which better describes my actions?

   _____ In a sinking ship, I would definitely be focused on getting my own life jacket.

   _____ In a sinking ship, I would instinctively be focused on helping others get to safety.

3. The last time I recall having an argument with someone, it was because _____ . In that situation, did I think about the other person's pain and frustration?

149

4. Instead of thinking about myself, I desire for God to help me think about:

What Were the Laborers Thinking?

Matthew 20:1–16

You're hot, thirsty, and absolutely exhausted. You've been in the vineyard since morning, and daybreak seems like a long time ago. Today was a scorcher, but the promise of a denarius kept you going. You feel grateful that you were picked for the work, and the time has now come to receive your reward.

It was an odd sort of day in the vineyard, because every few hours it seemed that new men kept showing up to pull a shift. At first you thought the steward would shoo them away as thieves who were trying to sneak into the vineyard and deceive the landowner that they, too, had been chosen for work. You had met slippery people like that before. But the steward was aware that the men were new and he kept putting them to work. Whatever. You suppose that maybe the landowner decided late in the day to increase the labor force to bring in a greater yield. As long as you get paid, what do you care?

Then the steward calls forward the men who came to the vineyard last. You nearly gasp when you see that he's handing each of them a denarius. What? Wow, the landowner must be feeling generous today! It's going to be your lucky day! If he's giving a whole denarius to these men, how much more is he going to give you? Tonight you're going to feast like a king with the wages that surely are coming to you.

But what's this? Surely there's been some kind of mistake. You speak up. No, your wage can't be a denarius if that's what the guys who hardly worked have been paid. You deserve more. In fact, you demand more! It's only fair! What an outrage! How can the landowner treat you this way? No matter that a denarius seemed fair enough this morning. Actually, it seemed fair enough in the heat of the day. But now that others less deserving than you are getting paid that amount, the deal is off. The landowner needs to see things from your perspective.

In this parable that Jesus told, the laborers could only think about what was happening to them. They couldn't appreciate the blessing being given to the late hires. They didn't respect the authority of the landowner. They could only think about how the payment system affected them, and they accused the landowner of being unfair.

In your efforts to love God with your mind, start thinking about the blessings that God wants to give others. Dwell on the authority of God to work in your life and the lives of others however He deems right, and respect His willingness to widely distribute His gifts of grace. Think less about you and more about others.

151

DAY 25: UNIQUELY YOU

Thought: God has given you specific gifts, skills, talents, and interests to fulfill His calling on your life.

Challenge: Let God help you figure out what He's suited you to do, then do it.

Abraham Lincoln once said, "If I only had an hour to chop down a tree, I would spend the first 45 minutes sharpening my axe." You only have one life to live, and a portion of it is already spent. Are you a sharpened tool in the hands of God?

You can spend your life dabbling in this and that and be mediocre at a little bit of everything, or you can focus your attention on gaining excellence in the specific calling God has for you. To truly soar, you have to know yourself.

- You need to know your spiritual gifts. To search out your giftedness, you've got to know the possibilities. Bible scholars disagree on how many specific spiritual gifts are listed in Scripture because the various listings have some overlap. But what is certain is that every Christian has been given at least one spiritual gift by the Holy Spirit, and that gift is to be used in service to the Lord.

  Many believers never exercise their spiritual gifts to their fullest potential because they're not sure what God has given them. Read through the passages that address spiritual gifts—such as Romans 12:3–8; 1 Corinthians 12; and Ephesians 4:7–16—and ask God to give you a clear understanding of your spiritual gifts. Once you know what He has gifted you to do, do it! *"Having then gifts differing according to the grace that is given to us, let us use them: if prophecy, let us prophesy in proportion to our faith; or ministry, let us use it in our ministering; he who teaches, in teaching; he who exhorts, in exhortation; he who gives, with liberality; he who leads, with diligence; he who shows mercy, with cheerfulness"* (Romans 12:6–8). Use your gifts with gusto.

- You need to know your talents. There's something very beautiful about watching a natural play baseball. He swings the bat with finesse. He throws the ball with strength and precision. His glove is like a ball magnet, and he instinctively plays the game. On the other hand, it's rather painful to observe someone trying to do a skill that they're not suited to do. Oh, we all appreciate the little chum in right field who couldn't catch a fly ball if his life depended on it, because he loves the game and he's a good sport for trying. But we're doing him a great disservice if we tell this child that he was born to be a ballplayer and he spends half his life working overtime to achieve a skill he doesn't have, when all the while he was born with the fingers to be the best piano player in the western hemisphere.

The mind either denies the truth or embraces it. You need an accurate knowledge of which skills God has given you; wanting to be good at something doesn't make it so. Abraham Lincoln also said, "Whatever you are, be a good one." It's a decision.

- You need to know your interests. In high school, I knew that math was one of my strengths, and I decided to pursue a career in it. I also knew that I wanted to make a big salary, so I decided to become an engineer. After entering college, I changed my major quickly from engineering to math education, because I couldn't stand the thoughts of sitting through several semesters of engineering courses. I just wasn't interested. Instead, I had a God-given interest to teach, and I'm grateful I was honest with myself before I wasted a lot of time and energy in a field that God hadn't chosen for me.

  God knitted you together in your mother's womb (Psalm 139:13), and each stitch was with purpose. It's OK to be interested in ministering to preschoolers more than any other age group. What isn't wise is to be interested in ministering to preschoolers but pour all of your energies into youth ministry because your friends are pressuring you to fill the position in the youth department. What discipline or area of ministry really awakens your interest?

- You need to know your calling. What is it that makes your heart sing? What is it that inspires you to stay up all night, make personal sacrifices, and work tirelessly just for the privilege of being involved? I have a friend that has a great passion for coaching football. His eyes light up when he talks about x's and o's. He gets a twinkle in his eyes when he tells his stories about Friday nights on the sidelines because he knows he's building character in those young men, and he loves every minute of it. It will never be just a job to him, because for him, it's his calling.

God's Spirit flows freely through us when we're fulfilling our calling. It's beautiful and true, like the sound of a bird's song that God has given him, and his song will bring glory to God. As a follower of Christ, you have a calling on your life.

Be sure of your calling, know your talents and interests, discover your spiritual gifts, and then pursue your life with vigor. Know who God has specifically called you to be. Mull it over in your mind.

154

Time to Think:

1. Have I ever asked God to help me know my spiritual gifts? Why or why not?

2. Do I know what I'm really good at? Am I strengthening those skills? Do I use those skills for God's glory?

3. Do I take the time to think about my interests? How can I use my interests to express my love for God?

155

4. Am I fulfilling my calling? How often do I use my mind to think honestly and thoroughly about God's calling for me?

5. In an effort to better know how God has specifically created me to glorify Him, a step I can take today is:

What Was Samson Thinking?

Judges 16

Samson's life began with such promise. The Angel of the Lord came to foretell his birth and declare that he would be a Nazarite, a judge of the Israelites, and the deliverer of His people. Samson's parents took great care to follow the Angel of the Lord's instructions, because they wanted to take no chance that their carelessness would interfere with their son reaching his full potential.

Samson was gifted. God had equipped him with superhuman strength that God granted him to equip Samson to be a military champion. No one could withstand his might. Samson also was gifted with the Spirit of the Lord, who began to move in Samson's life in his youth.

Samson had skill. He knew how to outfox his enemies and bring them to defeat. He was not only strong, but he was also an unstoppable warrior. He once killed 1,000 men with a donkey's jawbone as his only weapon.

Samson had a calling. It was foretold before his birth that he would be a significant figure in the life of the Israelite nation. He knew God's specific will for his life.

Unfortunately, Samson was also reckless. He blatantly broke the Nazarite vow. He disobeyed God's Word with his loose morals with women. He was arrogant and lost sight of the fact that his gifts, skills, and calling were not for his own pleasure but for God's glory and the good of God's people. God allowed Samson to suffer great pain and humiliation when he was captured by the Philistines, who took away his eyes and turned Samson into their dancing monkey. Samson's life could be described as a tragic waste of God-given potential.

Scripture doesn't tell us what Samson was thinking while he sat in fetters, weak and blind, but oh, the thoughts that might have haunted him. We might guess that Samson spent a lot of sleepless nights thinking about all that he had thrown away. He might have painstakingly tried to retrace his steps, to discover just what had led him to be so careless with his life. He may have wondered many times about what might have been, if he had only taken interest in fulfilling his calling and using his gifts and skills for God's glory. Perhaps Samson asked himself, "What was I thinking?"

Samson's life ended in a heap of regret. What are you doing with your life? Are you the person you want to be? Are you living up to your potential? Have you given thought to what God has given you to prepare you for greatness in His kingdom? Think about it now; Samson's story testifies that someday might be too late.

The Best Kind of Knowing

chapter six

For God gives wisdom and knowledge and joy
to a man who is good in His sight.
—ECCLESIASTES 2:26—

Wisdom and knowledge are gifts from God. These treasures can't be bought or sold, and much to the disgrace of popular opinion, we aren't the originators of knowledge and wisdom. Knowledge isn't about how much we've figured out, and wisdom isn't about how much we've evolved. To love God with our minds, we need knowledge and wisdom that comes from Him, educating us in the greatest knowing of all time: knowing God.

DAY 26: A DESTRUCTIVE IGNORANCE

Thought: The most important knowledge is knowledge of God; the result of not knowing the One True God is destruction.

Challenge: Determine to know God intimately.

As the sophisticated woman seated beside me read a magazine, her behavior stole my attention. She was studying an article on finding faith, and I inconspicuously read the subheadings enough to realize the writer was proposing New Age beliefs and many different paths to heaven. As her eyes fell upon a paragraph of particular importance to her, she ran her finger down the page, line by line, as if trying to absorb the meaning of the text. My heart was breaking as she soaked up false teachings.

As she and I began to talk, I soon discovered how enamored she had become with the owner of the magazine, revering her as a spiritual leader. I also learned that this woman beside me was a Christian. As I began to point out how the teachings in the magazine she was opening her mind to were contrary to Scripture, she was shocked; it had not occurred to her to compare the New Age teachings against Scripture. The questions began to pour out of her heart about the many other false teachings she had been friendly toward, and she thanked me for sharing with her. In one moment of truth, she suddenly realized how dangerous it is for Christians to navigate spirituality apart from a strong knowledge of God.

We do not want to be one of those persons that Paul describes in 2 Timothy 3:7, people who are "always learning and never able to come to the knowledge of the truth." The ideas of this current age teach us to look within ourselves for the answers, to be stronger, smarter, and self-sufficient. However, a quest for truth within ourselves will always lead to self-deception, because the heart is deceitful and desperately wicked (Jeremiah 17:9). But how many times have you heard the advice, "Follow your heart"? Bad, bad advice. Knowledge that comes from the world ends in destruction (Proverbs 14:12).

As we learn how to navigate this world, we can't be content to be ignorant; it's hard work, but we desperately need to seize the knowledge of the truth. God has proclaimed that His people are being destroyed *"for lack of knowledge"* (Hosea 4:6). God wasn't stating His concern for His people to be better informed about science and mathematics, economic strategies or war tactics, meditation techniques or the art of feng shui, and He certainly wasn't referring to a lack of street savvy among His people. What was the void God was charging against His people? *"There is no truth or mercy or knowledge of God in the land"* (Hosea 4:1). To know God in the sense of the Hebrew word goes well beyond a surface understanding, a mere acquaintance, or a respect and appreciation; this same word for "know" is also used in Scripture to refer to the intimate nature of a husband knowing his wife. Intimately, passionately, through study as well as experience, God would have His people filled with knowledge of who He is—that's the knowledge of the truth. God is truth.

The book of Hosea is filled with God's warnings for His people who take such little thought of Him. In Hosea, God likens His people to a bride who is in a covenant relationship with Him. The bride should be pursuing a deep knowledge of the Bridegroom, but instead, God said that His people were pursuing other interests: *"The spirit of harlotry is in their midst, and they do not know the LORD"* (Hosea 5:4). Spiritual harlotry— what a harsh yet completely accurate assessment! When we are pursuing a deep knowledge of any person, activity, art, trade, or trend more than we are pursuing an intimate knowledge of God, our Maker considers it spiritual betrayal.

Our world is filled with knowledge. We could devote ourselves to study history—the past tense—and never even scratch the surface of all that has been said or done. We could spend a lifetime

161

studying math and the sciences, but we would expire before we learned all that has already been discovered, not to mention the discoveries being made daily; our minds could not keep pace. And what of God? How could we even begin to understand all of who God is? Jesus spent a finite amount of time on this earth, but after writing an entire book about Jesus' life, John wrote, *"And there are also many other things that Jesus did, which if they were written one by one, I suppose that even the world itself could not contain the books that would be written"* (John 21:25). On this side of heaven, we could never know all there is to know about God, but the pursuit is worthy, and it's not futile. God has said, *"You will seek Me and find Me, when you search for Me with all your heart"* (Jeremiah 29:13). Seek knowledge of God, and He will reveal Himself to you.

Time to Think:

1. Am I flirting with any ideas or beliefs that aren't based on God's Word?

2. Am I pursuing other loves more than I'm pursuing God? Do I know more about my hobbies or trade than I do about God?

3. Proverbs 5:23 teaches that a wicked man will die *"for lack of instruction."* Where do I typically seek instruction? Is it reliable instruction?

4. Is there something about God that I would like to know more about?

163

5. Is there any fear in my heart when I think about digging deeper to know who God is and what His nature is?

6. Titus 1:15–16 warns about those who deceive themselves, believing they know God when they really don't: *"To those who are defiled and unbelieving nothing is pure; but even their mind and conscience are defiled. They profess to know God, but in works they deny Him, being abominable, disobedient, and disqualified for every good work."* How do my works confirm or deny that I know God?

If you have any doubt that you have a saving knowledge of God, visit page 190 with an open mind and seek to know the truth.

What Were the Chief Priests and Scribes Thinking?

Matthew 2:1–12

After Jesus was born in Bethlehem, magi from the East packed their bags for a long journey. God had placed a star in the sky, a sign that the Messiah had been born, and they would not miss this opportunity to meet the Promised One face-to-face. This was a noble quest, not for political schmoozing or fortune seeking; what they had packed matched their stated purpose: they were coming to worship Him. They had gold, frankincense, and myrrh for the King of the Jews, and they wanted to lay their gifts—and their hearts—at Jesus' feet.

164

Their travels first took them to Jerusalem, an obvious place to look for the Christ Child, because God had said He had chosen Jerusalem for Himself to place His name (1 Kings 11:36). They began inquiring about the location of the One born King of the Jews. When King Herod heard this news, he was troubled. *Another* king of the Jews? Not acceptable. Then Herod turned to the ones who should have known about this coming King, the chief priests and scribes. They told Herod about the prophecy that the Christ Child was to be born in Bethlehem. And with the sharing of that piece of information, the chief priests and scribes are no longer part of this story.

The Messiah was their King! Their Savior! The Son of God! If anyone should have been excited about meeting the long-awaited Christ Child, shouldn't it have been the chief priests and scribes? But no. The magi traveled to Bethlehem, roughly five miles from Jerusalem, with no new traveling companions. The chief priests and scribes must have yawned and went home.

These who were supposed to be men of God did not bother to travel to a neighboring town to seek God's Son. What were they thinking? How far is too far to meet the Savior? And what lengths will you go to that you might truly know Him?

DAY 27: KNOWING GOD'S WORD

Thought: The Bible is the great source of knowledge and wisdom that God has given to mankind.

Challenge: Delve deeply and often into God's Word to search out treasures to enrich your life and strengthen your mind.

165

There comes a time in every student's life when you learn the difference between knowing the material and "knowing" the material. The day the first exam was returned to us graded in freshman calculus, our professor informed the class that scanning the textbook and having a general idea of what the notes from class were about was not going to result in a passing grade in college. I learned that lesson, and I never forgot it. As I moved on to my next level of education, I remember taking seminary courses and memorizing literally dozens of pages of notes in order to do well on my exams. One day while huddled in a corner over my notes, I began to wonder why I was willing to spend hours upon hours to memorize notes to make an A on an exam, when I would spend only a fraction of that time studying God's Word, and not even memorizing it word for word the way I memorized my notes.

The answer was motivation. I was motivated to make an A. I was willing to work through the night, drop social activities, and even skip meals in order to reach my goal. I knew that if I didn't study, I would suffer the consequences. I was convicted that I needed a greater motivation to know God's Word and to realize that if I didn't study the Bible, I would suffer consequences. I made a decision that day that I would no longer begin studying for my exams each day until I had first studied God's Word with passion, expectation, and without rushing.

Nobody is going to ring your doorbell every Friday and hand you a letter grade to let you know how successfully you're navigating life. But little by little, the truth bears itself out, and we will receive the rewards—or suffer the consequences—from the amount of time we have devoted to studying God's Word. Ninety-two percent of American households have at least one copy of the Christian Bible. Among Bible readers, the average amount of time spent reading the Bible in a week is 52 minutes.

Second Timothy 3:16–17 tells us what kind of value the Book holds: *"All Scripture is inspired by God and profitable for teaching, for reproof, for correction, for training in righteousness; so that the man of God may be adequate, equipped for every good work"* (NASB). Let's break it down:

- The Bible is God-breathed. Sunsets and stellar speeches can inspire, but only God can breathe life-giving words onto the pages of His Book and nourish us with every syllable.

- The Bible is the textbook of life. Want to know about God? Read the Bible. Want to know about mankind? Read the Bible. Want to know about eternity past, present, and future? Read the Bible. Want to know wisdom that cannot fail? Read it. It's more than a textbook, because every word is true and cannot be changed or challenged.

- The Bible sets the bar. For reproof and correction to take place, we line up our actions, attitudes, and thoughts beside Scripture, and we see where our crooked places are. Without absolute truth, we could never say with assurance that we were completely right or utterly wrong. We need to know the truth, and God has recorded the standard in His Word.

- The Bible trains us to get it right. We need to know the ways of Christ to follow in His footsteps, and we need the words of Scripture to help us each day as we remain in training to be right with God, to be more like Christ today than we were yesterday.

- The Bible fills every slot in the tool belt. If we're going to live successfully for God, we need to be equipped with tools for life. The Bible prepares us to do God's work.

167

You may have already known every one of those points about Scripture. You may agree with every point. You may have 2 Timothy 3:16–17 memorized! But do you *know* God's Word?

Jeremiah 15:16 is the ideal approach to Scripture: *"Your words were found, and I ate them, and Your word was to me the joy and rejoicing of my heart; for I am called by Your name, O Lord God of hosts."* When we love God with our minds by partaking of God's Word, He will grant us great satisfaction in reading Scripture. Every word will taste like honeycomb. The pages will make our hearts joyful!

Time to Think:

1. The amount of time I spend each day reading the Bible:

2. The circumstances that cause me not to read the Bible on any given day include:

3. Beyond casual reading, I would like to know God's Word better by taking this step:
   _____ Memorizing verses
   _____ Reading through the Bible chronologically
   _____ Reading key passages over and over and recording my thoughts
   _____ Remaining in constant prayer while I'm reading and asking God to teach and convict me
   _____ Other: _____

4. *Therefore lay aside all filthiness and overflow of wickedness, and receive with meekness the implanted word, which is able to save your souls. But be doers of the word, and not hearers only, deceiving yourselves. For if anyone is a hearer of the word and not a doer, he is like a man observing his natural face in a mirror; for he observes himself, goes away, and immediately forgets what kind of man he was. But he who looks into the perfect law of liberty and continues in it,*

and is not a forgetful hearer but a doer of the work, this one will be blessed in what he does. (James 1:21–25).

a What do I have to lay aside to fully receive God's Word?

b. Do I approach God's Word with meekness? Do I long to study and understand God's Word with the humility and zeal of a person who knows she is hopeless apart from God?

c. After reading God's Word, am I deceiving myself by not heeding God's Word?

d. Am I consistent to continue in God's Word?

169

5. How does my appreciation for God's Word match that of the psalmist in Psalm 19:7–14?

What Were the Disciples Thinking?

Luke 24:13–53

It had been three days, and they were still talking it out, spinning the details around in their brains, trying to make sense of it all. Their mighty Prophet, Teacher, and Friend was ripped from their world in a whirlwind of events. It was still too soon, the wound too fresh, and they couldn't stop thinking about Jesus. He had said so many things that didn't seem to make sense at the time; was there a clue in those teachings that could help them understand? And why did Jesus have to die? It was going to be so beautiful when Jesus restored Israel, and all would've been perfect! But His untimely death had dashed their hopes.

Perhaps it was therapeutic for Cleopas to get to tell this Stranger about Jesus and the events that had taken place. Cleopas was free to tell the details that everyone else was growing weary of thinking about in their pain and sorrow. But then this Stranger stopped listening and was now talking; His talk was deep and sweet as He reached back into the beginning of history and spoke with an authority and vigor that enraptured Cleopas's mind. And then at the evening meal when the Stranger revealed Himself to be none other than Jesus the Risen Savior— oh, the wonder of it all! Cleopas, of all people. Jesus had chosen to appear to him and opened up his understanding!

As Cleopas and his disciple friend hurried to Jerusalem to tell the other eleven what happened, he found them already in a stir, for the Lord had also appeared to Simon! Then their dizzied state was magnified because at that very moment, Jesus Himself appeared with a simple yet profound statement: *"Peace to you"* (v. 36).

But no, they would have no peace, only terror, trouble, and doubt. Jesus showed them His nail-scarred hands and feet, but they still did not believe for joy. Their minds could not understand what their eyes were telling them. *How could this be?* Then Jesus began to speak the words that would change their minds. *"Now He said to them, 'These are My words which I spoke to you while I was still with you, that all things which are written about Me in the Law of Moses and the Prophets and the Psalms must be fulfilled.' Then He opened their minds to understand the Scriptures"* (vv. 44–45 NASB).

Their minds had been narrow—so narrow that they couldn't even believe what they could see, but the Lord opened up their minds to understand God's Holy Word. Imagine the rush of joy and gratitude when all the puzzle pieces began to lock into place as Jesus explained God's plan of redemption by marching through Scripture.

171

Do you need understanding as you open God's Word? Ask the Lord to be your Teacher.

DAY 28: SPIRITUAL RADAR

Thought: Discernment requires Spirit-filled thinking that examines matters with God's eyes.

Challenge: Ask God for discernment.

Discernment seems to bring a calming peace to God's people in the face of trials and decisions. Elisha, whose nickname was "man of God," seemed to positively drip with discernment. God revealed to Elisha the schemes of Israel's enemies, and when the evil king of Aram learned that he had Elisha to thank for all of his thwarted plots, he sent horses, chariots, and a great army to Dothan where Elisha was sleeping. By dawn, the city was surrounded, and Elisha's servant quivered at the sight. *"Alas, my master! What shall we do?" So he answered, "Do not fear, for those who are with us are more than those who are with them." Then Elisha prayed and said, "'O LORD, I pray, open his eyes that he may see.' And the LORD opened the servant's eyes and he saw; and behold, the mountain was full of horses and chariots of fire all around Elisha"* (2 Kings 6:15–17 NASB). God had given Elisha a glimpse of His active presence in His life, and this gave Elisha a confidence about what to do in the face of his enemies.

Discernment, whether it's the kind of miraculous experiences that Elisha had or the whispers of God that we receive for daily living, is a powerful kind of thinking. It's knowing that an organization may not have the motives they advertise. It's sensing that something is wrong at school even though your daughter insists everything is fine. It's going left at the fork of decision even though the path to the right is lush and green, because God is clearly pointing left. Spiritual discernment is the ability to make decisions by examining a situation thoroughly, as if with the eyes of God to penetrate beyond what is plainly seen, to know the truth based on God's wisdom. It's spiritual radar.

Discernment is not for every man, because God must grant this gift of privilege. Scripture gives us insight into spiritual discernment.

- Discernment belongs to God. Only He is able to see every situation in past, present, and future. Only He knows the inner thoughts and intentions of every person. God is able to look at one decision in your life and know how thousands of people will be affected in the ripples of your choice, how your future decisions will be swayed by this outcome, and how His ultimate plan for your life is designed to go. The Lord is not limited the way we are. To gather information, we have only our senses, which are often deceived, but the Lord *"shall not judge by the sight of His eyes, nor decide by the hearing of His ears"* (Isaiah 11:3).

- Discernment is given to God's people (1 Corinthians 2:14). The "natural man," or the person who has not been transformed by God through salvation in Jesus Christ, is not capable of seizing spiritual wisdom. Without God's Spirit within us, trying to catch all the facts to discern the truth is like capturing broth with a fork; most of what you seek eludes you. The Holy Spirit within every believer plays an active role in our ability to discern, for He holds the wisdom of the deep layers of God (vv. 10–13).

  Paul says in Ephesians 4 that without Christ, the mind is fixated on futility (v. 17), understanding is darkened (v. 18), and ignorance and blindness separate the unbeliever from God (v. 18). But the world is filled with brilliant minds that lead nations, discover cures, and save companies. Surely that takes discernment, right? There's no arguing that God allows people who do not honor him to achieve great things in this world; otherwise, people would be signing up left and right to be Christians to assure their success on this earth. On the contrary, there is a discernment of this world—resulting in media sensations, business moxie, million dollar hunches, or the like—but without Christ, our discernment is limited to know only that which is of this world. You cannot see through God's eyes until you know God.

- Our desire for discernment should be with noble intent. When Solomon became king of Israel, he asked for wisdom *"that I*

173

may discern between good and evil" (1 Kings 3:9). Solomon's request was not for discernment to benefit himself or impress the kingdom, but to better serve God by serving others. Our motive shouldn't be to wow the crowds with our great abilities to discern, but to be an effective decision maker for God's glory.

• Spiritual discernment comes with practice as we mature in Christ. God can grant discernment in an instant as He did for King Solomon, but in Hebrews, we're instructed that discernment also comes to *"the mature, who because of practice have their senses trained to discern good and evil"* (5:14 NASB).

When it comes to spiritual discernment, the power of knowing is not the power of solving. As we begin to spiritually discern, the weight of the truth brings us to our knees in prayer. We can't fix people, nor is it our place to show up their weaknesses. Corrie ten Boom said, "Discernment is God's call to intercession, never to faultfinding." We pray because God can positively transform their lives, so we turn their faulty ways over to His capable hands. And as we pray, God illuminates our minds to know how to be His instrument to bring peace and reveal the truth.

Time to Think:

1. Do I value discernment? Do I long to see my world through God's eyes?

2. Who are the discerning people in my life? What is the evidence of their discernment?

3. Do I typically fall into traps of sin or deception? Are there areas in my life where I am more discerning than others?

4. When I think about my relationships or situations, do I usually look through my own eyes, or do I call out to God to let me see through His eyes?

5. Am I praying with discernment?

What Was Rehoboam Thinking?

1 Kings 12:1–16

King Solomon was the wisest man who ever lived. How would his son Rehoboam compare as king? When the time had come for Rehoboam to reign, he traveled to Shechem where the people had gathered to make him king. This would be a grand affair! But the people had more on their minds than celebration of their king. They stated their case before him, hoping that the first act of his reign would be to lighten their burden. There was no way for Rehoboam to anticipate this request right out of the gate. What would he do, being put on the spot? Rehoboam was young and inexperienced, but perhaps it was a glimmer of wisdom that he sent them away for three days before he would make his decision. God could accomplish many a thing in three days, even in a young king like Rehoboam.

The young king consulted two parties: his father's elders and his childhood buddies. The elders' advice displeased him; *be a servant to the people?* No. So Rehoboam adopted the plan of his young friends, to oppress the people and issue great threats. What was running through that young man's mind? Perhaps Rehoboam thought, *I am the king, aren't I? It's my time now. I will not be told what to do—not by the people, and not by these elders who think they know better than me. I will put my thumbprint on these people, and they will obey me.*

And that's just what Rehoboam did. He pressed down with his thumb, and the people countermoved with a scenario Rehoboam had not anticipated: They rejected him as king. The kingdom of Israel was torn asunder, and Rehoboam would never reign over the entirety of his father's kingdom.

Rehoboam made a history-altering mistake. He looked at the decision through the eyes of the elders, but he didn't like what they saw. He considered the view from where he and his young friends were standing, and he lunged on a choice that looked good at the time. Rehoboam could not discern the situation because he didn't seek God's perspective. He didn't ask God to fill his mind with the truth. Rehoboam couldn't blame the people, nor his friends, nor his youth and inexperience. Rehoboam had only himself to blame, because he did not seek spiritual discernment. He did not seek to see the kingdom through God's eyes.

DAY 29: UNSEARCHABLE MYSTERIES

Thought: God—who He is and what He does—is beyond human comprehension.

Challenge: Accept that you cannot explain God.

Think about your sixth birthday. How much do you remember? Now go back to the day you were born. Tell us what happened. What were you thinking when you first felt the touch of your mother's hand? Think back 2,000 years. What do you know about the day Jesus was born? Retreat thousands of years, to the time when the Spirit hovered over the waters, and the earth was without form and void. Now go back in time some more. More, more, keep going . . . and at some point your brain just can't do it anymore. Our brains are conditioned to think linearly about time. We cannot comprehend eternity.

In fact, we can't even produce a complete listing of all the mysteries of this universe that we can't explain. Our knowledge is so limited that we don't even know the extent of what we don't know. Gifted scientists like Stephen Hawking have a jump on the rest of us in making that list, as he and other brilliant scientific minds have set their mark to explain the universe. However, one of the flaws of a limited mind is fooling ourselves into thinking we know more than God. Hawking has concluded, "Spontaneous creation is the reason there is something rather than nothing, why the universe exists, why we exist. It is not necessary to invoke God." Spontaneous creation, many would argue, takes more faith than believing in God, and the mysteries of the universe don't even begin to complete the list of all that we do not and cannot know about the world, time, space, humanity, and most importantly: God.

Great men who walked with the Lord have said this about the mysteries of God:

- *"The secret things belong to the LORD our God"* (Deuteronomy 29:29 NASB). God talked to Moses from a burning bush, God showed Moses His glory, and *"the LORD spoke to Moses face to face, as a man speaks to his friend"* (Exodus 33:11). Moses was intimately acquainted with the God of this universe, yet Moses knew there was more to the identity of God than he could ever know.

- *"He has made everything beautiful in its time. Also He has put eternity in their hearts, except that no one can find out the work that God does from beginning to end"* (Ecclesiastes 3:11). Solomon had more wisdom than any other human had ever had or will have because it was God's gift to him. In his wisdom, Solomon knew that even he couldn't uncover all of the works of God.

178

- *"Have you not known? Have you not heard? The everlasting God, the LORD, the Creator of the ends of the earth, neither faints nor is weary. His understanding is unsearchable"* (Isaiah 40:28). Isaiah had amazing prophecies revealed to him directly by God. They were prophecies of things to come, details about the Messiah, the Son of God. What an outpouring of great knowledge from God! Isaiah knew things that had not been revealed to any other man, yet Isaiah knew that God's grasp on all that has been and all that will be is beyond man's search.

- *"Oh, the depth of the riches both of the wisdom and knowledge of God! How unsearchable are His judgments and His ways past finding out"* (Romans 11:33)! Paul had a personal visit from Jesus to reveal the truth to him and save his soul. Paul wrote 13 epistles, nearly one-fourth of the New Testament, that have helped shaped the theology of the Christian church. Paul was given wisdom that extends well beyond the common man, writing the epistles with confidence that God was directing each word, and all the while declaring that God's ways are beyond discovery.

179

These great men and many more like them knew so much about God and yet declared that they knew so little. They came face-to-face with their limitations, and they accepted with unshakable faith that God was beyond their comprehension.

I'm grateful that God is beyond my ability to understand or explain, for He is holding me while He also holds the planets in orbit. In His words, He is the great I AM. And yet, while He cannot be reduced to human size, He came to dwell among us. He will not be contained in books but He has filled a Book with revelation of who He is, what He has done, and what He is doing. And in His great Book, the Holy Bible, we are told that *"now we see in a mirror, dimly, but then face to face. Now I know in part, but then I shall know just as I also am known"* (1 Corinthians 13:12). There is coming a day when *"we shall see Him as He is"* (1 John 3:2).

If you have questions about God, you aren't the first person and you won't be the last. It's OK to ask God with an honest heart, as long as you understand that God is under no obligation to answer you. Loving God with your mind means seeking to know Him more each day, and being content with mysteries He chooses to keep behind the veil.

Time to Think:

1. My attempt to describe the greatness of God:

2. How often do I think on the unsearchable mysteries of God?
   _____ I have a lot of questions.
   _____ I don't spend a lot of time thinking about it.
   _____ I love to think about how wondrous God is.

3. When confronted with a question about God I can't answer, I tend to:
   _____ Doubt in my mind.
   _____ Pray about it.
   _____ Worship God for being so great and mighty.

181

4. When tragedies happen and people start doubting God, I will love God with my mind by:

5. Of all the verses contained in today's chapter, the one that means the most to me is _____ because:

What Was Jeremiah Thinking?

Jeremiah 12:1–17

It wasn't easy being Jeremiah. When God called him to be a prophet in his youth, God told Jeremiah that He would face persecution. In his ministry Jeremiah dealt with corrupt priests, false prophets, wicked kings, and hardhearted kinsmen living in ignorance. Jeremiah delivered God's messages of rebuke and impending destruction day after day through many seasons, but his pleadings with the people largely fell on deaf ears. Jeremiah's integrity as a prophet was questioned, and he was even imprisoned, yet he continued to deliver the messages of God.

Jeremiah was a mighty man of God, but Jeremiah was also just a man. He was privileged to talk with God, but Jeremiah had many unanswered questions. One day Jeremiah came before the Lord with a rather bold question: *"Righteous are You, O LORD, that I would plead my case with You; indeed I would discuss matters of justice with You: Why has the way of the wicked prospered? Why are all those who deal in treachery at ease"* (12:1 NASB)? Jeremiah didn't accuse God of poor judgment, but he did question God's rationale.

Have you ever felt like asking God, "Lord, what are You doing? Why are You letting this happen?" There is indeed a lot of injustice in this world. It appears that evil goes unpunished. The wicked sometimes get richer while the faithful struggle. Righteous people suffer no less than people who take no thought of God. Why does God let His children suffer? Why do the evil get to smirk at their victims while the righteous cry out?

God has said, *"'My thoughts are not your thoughts, nor are your ways My ways'"* (Isaiah 55:8). God is on His throne, allowing people to make choices that they will be accountable for in the final judgment. God is a righteous Judge, and we can trust in His judgments on the day of reckoning. In the meantime, God still reigns. Sometimes He intervenes (and in those times we often do not know what tragedies the world has been spared,) and sometimes He applies grace to those who are suffering. Regardless of what He does both seen and unseen, God is good.

We can put ourselves in Jeremiah's shoes and understand why a man in the throes of dealing with stubborn wickedness would ask the Lord to help him make sense of it all. And how could God help one man understand how the events of his lifetime would have eternal consequences for a nation of people and beyond? But God is patient with us. Even this I do not understand.

183

DAY 30: WHO HE IS AND WHAT HE PROMISED

Thought: Satan will attack the minds of believers and unbe-lievers, telling lies and trying to raise doubts about God and His promises.

Challenge: Let your mind become a fortress of God's truth, solid in your faith in who God is and what He has promised.

We're coming to the end of our 30-day journey. What have you learned about God? What have you learned about yourself? I hope you've expanded your ability to love God with your mind, and you feel prepared to exercise your thought life for the glory of God. Now walk your unfamiliar road with a mind set free in God's sweet love.

If you're going to continue to love God with your mind, you're going to have a fight on your hands. If you've carefully examined your mind and sought to employ what you've learned in the past 29 days, then you already know that Satan and his minions are attacking on every front of the mind, and he is looking for any possible ploy to weaken your faith. You're going to have to be fiercely determined to have a steely mind that refuses to be weakened by deception.

Lies are in Satan's arsenal, and deception is his game. He throws around half-truths as well as whopping lies, and he knows we'll weaken if we doubt what God has said. It worked for him in the garden when he deceived Adam and Eve. He hissed, "'Did God really say . . . ?'", and the next thing we know, Adam and Eve both had a mouthful.

What Satan began in the beginning, he continues today. He attacked the early Christians with deception. Paul had to write a letter to the Christians in Thessalonica because they had become "shaken in mind" with lies being spread that Jesus had already come and not received them (2 Thessalonians 2:1–3). As time marches on, Satan's deceptions will only heighten, and your mind will be challenged. Your faith will not waiver and your mind will be unshaken if you're sure of what you know about who God is and what He has promised. Hold fast to these truths:

- Jesus is the Christ, the Messiah, the Son of the Living God. When Jesus faced the Sanhedrin during His trial, they asked Him if He was the Son of God. Jesus replied, *"You rightly say that I am'"* (Luke 22:70). He performed miracles, received worship, told the Samaritan woman that He was the Messiah (John 4:26), declared that He was the great I AM (8:58), and said that He was One with the Father (10:30). Jesus had full awareness of His divinity, and He knew that He had come to the earth to give His life as a sacrifice (Matthew 16:21; Mark 10:45; John 10:17–18).

- Jesus is the only way of salvation. Jesus declared, *"I am the way, the truth, and the life. No one comes to the Father except through Me'"* (John 14:6). Jesus knew that He was the gateway to salvation. Deceivers declare that such narrow thinking is nothing less than bigotry. There is no unkindness in God that He offers only one way. The mercy and kindness of God is that He offers mankind any way at all.

- God loves you. Yes, you may be a little less lovable to your friends on some days more than others. All of us have difficult days. God's love for you is not in any way increased or decreased by your thoughts, beliefs, or actions. *"But God demonstrates His own love toward us, in that while we were still sinners, Christ died for us"* (Romans 5:8). On your worst day, God loves you with an eternal love that is unscathed by your sin. As a believer, your sin creates a barrier of communication (Psalm 66:18), but nothing can separate you from God's love (Romans 8:39).

- God will never leave you. God has promised to *"never leave you nor forsake you"* (Hebrews 13:5). No matter how lonely you may feel for human companionship, you will never want for the companionship of God Himself. In the darkest night or the fiercest storm, God will be with you.

- Jesus is coming again. Jesus said, *"I will come again and receive you to Myself; that where I am, there you may be also'"* (John 14:3). In Revelation 22, the last chapter of the last

185

book of the Bible, Jesus said, *"I am coming quickly'"* (vv. 7, 12, 20). The passing of time doesn't make Jesus' words less true; it makes our expectations heightened as we know the day approaches.

These and many more are the promises of God. Know these truths and keep them before you. Strengthen your mind with fortresses of truth built on the foundation of Jesus Christ. Stand on the fortress armed with wisdom and faith, and love God with your mind.

Time to Think:

1. Why does Satan try to deceive people about Jesus? What are his tactics?

2. When Satan attacks me with lies, sometimes:
   _____ I am weakened when I don't pay attention to my thought life; I fail to be mindful of Christ in my life.
   _____ I am tempted to cave to pressure when people around me ridicule Christianity.
   _____ I allow sorrow and circumstances to cause me to doubt God's love for me.
   _____ I find myself listening to his lie: "Did God really say ... ?"
   _____ Other: _____

3. I will stand on God's promises. Today I will stay mindful of this particular promise of God:

4. Ephesians 4:21 teaches that *"the truth is in Jesus."* With God's help, this is what I know to be true:

187

What Was Thomas Thinking?

John 20:24–29

He wasn't going to be jerked around. He was too fragile. He couldn't take another disappointment. He had placed his faith in the great Teacher Jesus, certain that this Man was the Son of God, the promised King of Israel. But a cruel cross had been the end of Jesus of Nazareth, and Thomas was still sorting through scraps of memories. What had gone wrong? And what was to come of him and the other men and women committed to serve Jesus, now that He was gone? The Sanhedrin would keep peddling their man-made religion, and the Romans would continue to keep Israel under Caesar's thumb. As Jesus performed miracles and taught the people, it had seemed that everything was going to change; Thomas knew that his life had been changed by Jesus. But now . . . ? But now his hope had been buried in a tomb and a stone was rolled at the entrance.

The other disciples came to Thomas with incredible news. They had seen the Lord! He was risen from the dead! Wonder and rejoicing should have overtaken each one of them, but Thomas would have no part in the celebration. "Unless I see the nail marks in his hands, and also touch them, along with touching His pierced side, I will not believe."

Jesus appeared, and before Thomas could ask, Jesus told him specifically to touch the scars in his hands and side. Jesus already knew Thomas's mind, and He met Thomas at his point of doubt. Thomas responded with worship of the risen Lord. Thomas was now convinced that Jesus was Lord. History tells us that he never again wavered from this truth and eventually gave his life for his faith in Jesus Christ. Every person, like Thomas, must decide if he will believe.

How to Become a Christian

God desires to have a personal relationship with you.
"For I know the thoughts that I think toward you,' says the LORD, 'thoughts of peace and not of evil, to give you a future and a hope'" (Jeremiah 29:11).

But our sin separates us from God. All of us are sinners; no one can live up to God's holy standard, which is perfection.
"For all have sinned and fall short of the glory of God" (Romans 3:23).

The penalty we deserve for our sin is spiritual death—total separation from God in hell.
"For the wages of sin is death, but the gift of God is eternal life in Christ Jesus our Lord" (Romans 6:23).

God is offering you the gift of eternal life through Jesus Christ.
"For God so loved the world that He gave His only begotten Son, that whoever believes in Him should not perish but have everlasting life" (John 3:16).

Jesus Christ is the Son of God. He is the one and only bridge to God.
Jesus said, *"I am the way, the truth, and the life. No one comes to the Father except through me'"* (John 14:6).

Jesus lived a sinless life. He allowed Himself to be nailed to the Cross to pay the price for our sins so we would not have to face hell. What a wonderful act of love! He died on the Cross, was buried, and then rose from the grave.

"But God demonstrates His own love toward us, in that while we were still sinners, Christ died for us" (Romans 5:8).

God is offering you new life in Jesus Christ. Do you want to become a Christian? Then through prayer to God:

1. Admit you are a sinner, asking for forgiveness and turning from your sins.

2. Confess that Jesus, the Son of God, died on the Cross and rose again to save you from your sins.

3. Invite Jesus to be the Lord and Savior of your life.

Dear God, I know that I am a sinner. I am asking for Your forgiveness, and I want to turn away from my sins. I believe that Jesus, Your Son, died on the Cross and rose again to save me from my sins, and I now put my trust in Him as my personal Lord and Savior. Amen.

"Whoever calls on the name of the LORD shall be saved" (Romans 10:13).

If you have prayed to receive Christ, you have been given forgiveness and eternal life!

Your
eDevotional for use with
Lost on a Familiar Road

Find out more at **NewHopeDigital.com**

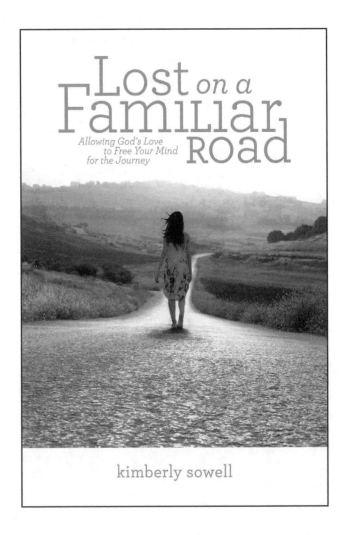

Get more out of your reading experience with free book-club guides,
small-group study guides, and more at NewHopeDigital.com

---

*New Hope® Publishers is a division of WMU®, an international
organization that challenges Christian believers to understand and be
radically involved in God's mission. For more information about WMU,
go to wmu.com. More information about New Hope books may be found at
NewHopeDigital.com. New Hope books may be
purchased at your local bookstore.*

Use the QR reader on your
smartphone to visit us online at
NewHopeDigital.com

If you've been blessed by this book, we would like to hear your story.
The publisher and author welcome your comments and
suggestions at: newhopereader@wmu.org.